A WALKIN
PAF

Sketches of the city's architectural treasures...

Journey through the urban landscape of Paris

Gregory Byrne Bracken

Marshall Cavendish Editions

All text and illustrations by G. Byrne Bracken
Editor: Stephanie Yeo
Designer: Benson Tan

Published in 2012 by Marshall Cavendish Business
An imprint of Marshall Cavendish International

PO Box 65829
London EC1P 1NY
United Kingdom
info@marshallcavendish.co.uk

and

1 New Industrial Road, Singapore 536196
genrefsales@marshallcavendish.com
www.marshallcavendish.com/genref

Other Marshall Cavendish offices:
Marshall Cavendish International (Asia) Private Limited, 1 New Industrial Road,
Singapore 536196 · Marshall Cavendish Corporation, 99 White Plains Road, Tarrytown,
NY 10591 · Marshall Cavendish International (Thailand) Co Ltd. 253 Asoke, 12th Flr,
Sukhumvit 21 Road, Klongtoey Nua, Wattana, Bangkok 10110, Thailand · Marshall
Cavendish (Malaysia) Sdn Bhd, Times Subang, Lot 46, Subang Hi-Tech Industrial Park,
Batu Tiga, 40000 Shah Alam, Selangor Darul Ehsan, Malaysia

Marshall Cavendish is a trademark of Times Publishing Limited

A CIP record for this book is available from the British Library

ISBN 978 981 4351 24 9

Printed and bound in Singapore by KWF Printing Pte Ltd

This book is dedicated to Johann and Noël Wilbrenninck.

Contents

Acknowledgments

I would like first of all to thank Melvin Neo and Martin Liu at Marshall Cavendish for their wonderful support on this project. Also the editor Stephanie Yeo and the designer Benson Tan who do such hard work in making these books as good as they are. Thanks also to Robert Cortlever, Cathinca Cortlever and Jasper Folmer for being such pleasant companions on the first of my research trips to Paris, and my mother, Maura Bracken, for the second. In fact thanks go to both my mother and my father, Brendan Bracken, for allowing me the chance to go to school in Paris all those years ago; the time I spent at College Franklin (St Louis de Gonzague) was magical.

My heartiest thanks must go to Johann and Noël Wilbrenninck for all the extra titbits of fascinating information they gave, and the warm welcome every time I get to see them at home in France. Thanks also to Patrick Healy for his excellent tips and suggestions, as on all my various projects, your advice is invaluable. And a big thank you to the Delft School of Design, particularly Arie Graafland and Deborah Hauptmann, and the International Institute for Asian Studies in Leiden, especially Manon Osseweijer and Philippe Peycam, without whom I could do none of this work. I would also like to thank Jan Beer for telling me the history of the term 'bistrot', and Casper van der Kruk for the Castel Bérenger/Déranger anecdote.

Suggested Itineraries

Historical
The Islands
Le Marais
Latin Quarter
Jardin des Plantes

Cultural
Le Marais
Beaubourg
Tuileries
Latin Quarter
Opéra
Montmartre

Shopping
Le Marais
Tuileries
St-Germain-des-Prés
Champs-Elysées
Opéra

Markets
The Islands
Opéra
Further Afield

Nightlife
St-Germain-des-Prés
Champs-Elysées
Opéra
Montmartre

Children's
Tuileries
Jardin des Plantes
Montparnasse
Trocadéro
Further Afield

Introduction

As a city, Paris needs no introduction. Beloved of artists, writers and thinkers, not to mention lovers, it is as famous for its fashion as its food – both of which are world class – and of course its art and architecture. Paris is full of wonderful places to experience: from the magnificence of the Louvre and the Musée d'Orsay to tiny little museums dedicated to artists and writers dotted throughout the city, such as the Musée Gustave Moreau or the Musée Zadkine. The city is also home to ancient Roman ruins, with Roman baths at Cluny and the Arènes de Lutèce, an arena where gladiators fought to the death.

Paris is justifiably famous for its Gothic architecture, including some of the masterpieces of the style, including Notre-Dame Cathedral and the Sainte-Chapelle. Then there are the stunning *hôtels particuliers*, aristocratic town houses, such as the Hôtel de Lauzun or the Hôtel de Soubise, many of which are open to the public to catch a glimpse of life as an aristocrat before the French Revolution. Paris is also home to cutting-edge modern architecture, with the Pompidou Centre and La Villette as well as, of course, the world-famous Pyramid of the Louvre.

The city is also surprisingly green, with numerous parks and squares, including the delightful Jardin du Luxembourg and the Tuileries, not to mention the famous tree-lined boulevards laid out by Baron Haussmann in the 19th century. Avenue de l'Opéra and the Champs-Elysées are thronged with *flâneurs* wanting to see and be seen. For a bird's-eye view, climb the Eiffel Tower, where you can take in the entire city spread out beneath your feet. You can also enjoy spectacular views from the soaring Tour Montparnasse or from Sacré-Coeur in Montmartre.

The walks in this book have been arranged according to the different city districts, such as the Latin Quarter or the Opéra. Each one starts where the previous one left off, and there are 14 in all. Starting at the historical islands at the centre of Paris, they work their way around the various neighbourhoods to end in Montmartre. There is also a Further Afield chapter which takes in the buildings and places that fall a little outside the city centre. This is followed by a chapter which explains the various architectural styles mentioned in the book, and a listings section that includes contact details, there is also a glossary of architectural terms. Finally, there is even a short introduction to the French language to help you on your way.

All that remains is to wish you a pleasant time strolling around one of the world's most magical cities.

Notes

History of Paris

Some of the world's most important architectural developments were made in Paris, from the lightness of the Gothic style (at the Basilica of St-Denis) to the Modernist villas of Le Corbusier. Both of these styles have a lot in common, in fact, as they are both premised on the principle of spacious uncluttered interiors and the allowance of the maximum amount of light. Gothic's huge windows were divided by only the slimmest of stone tracery which gave it the effect of a wall of glass, something remarkably similar to the curtain wall of Modernism centuries later.

Paris' patron saint is Sainte Geneviève, a wealthy 5th-century Gallo-Roman landowner who gathered her friends together to pray that the city would be spared when Huns invaded in 451 CE. Their prayers were answered and there is a shrine to her in St-Etienne-du-Mont, on the appropriately named Place Ste-Geneviève, as well as a statue of her by Michel-Louis Victor, from 1845, in the Jardin du Luxembourg.

Paris may be famous for its Gothic architecture, but it also has a strong affinity with Ancient Greece and Rome, and many of the city's place names reflect this. The Champs-Elysées (Elysian Fields – a sort of heaven in ancient Greece), the Champ-de-Mars (Field of Mars – the Roman god of war – a poetic term for battlefield) is the name of the old military drilling ground between the Eiffel Tower and the Ecole Militaire, not to mention Montparnasse (Mount Parnassus), Apollo's sacred mountain and home of the muses. Apollo was also the icon of King Louis XIV who sought to emulate the Greek god when he crowned himself Sun King – the palace of Versailles and its gardens revel in Apollonian imagery.

The capital and largest city in France, Paris straddles the River Seine and sits at the heart of the region known as the Ile-de-France. Estimated to have a population of well over two million, the city's wider metropolis is home to almost 12 million. One of the world's most popular tourist destinations, the city receives approximately 45 million visitors a year.

The earliest evidence of permanent settlement dates from around 4200 BCE, and a Celtic tribe known as the Parisii were said to have lived here around 250 BCE. The Romans under Julius Caesar then conquered the region in 53 BCE and established a city on Ile de la Cité that stretched as far as Place Ste-Geneviève. Originally called Lutetia, this was later changed to the more French-sounding Lutèce. With the collapse of the Roman empire in the 5th century, the city was invaded by Germanic tribes and fell into decline, shrinking to a small fortified garrison on the island. This was when it changed its name back to Paris.

The city remained under the control of the Germanic Franks from the late 5th century onwards, with King Clovis founding the Merovingian dynasty and establishing the city as his capital in 508. By the late 8th century the Carolingian dynasty took over and moved their Frankish capital to Aachen in Germany.

This coincided with a series of vicious Viking raids lasting well into the 9th century. The raids forced Parisians to build a strong fortress on the Ile de la Cité.

As the power of the Carolingian kings waned, the Count of Paris, Hugh Capet, had himself elected King of France in 987 and turned Paris into his capital city. It fell to the English during the Hundred Years' War but was restored to French rule in 1436 under Charles VII. The city remained the country's capital only in name, however, as the real power lay in the Loire Valley. François I re-established the city as a royal home in 1528.

During the Wars of Religion, Paris was a Roman Catholic stronghold, but on 24 August 1572 it experienced one of its most infamous events. Margaret of Valois, sister of the Catholic King Charles IX, was due to marry the Protestant Henri of Navarre. Protestants were encouraged to come to the city and celebrate, but once there they were brutally slaughtered. The St. Bartholomew's Day Massacre was a low point in the city's history. Henri of Navarre eventually became King Henri IV but was forced to convert to Catholicism to do so and famously said 'Paris is worth a mass'. He did much to beautify the city. His grandson Louis XIV also did a lot to embellish the city, but was responsible for even more outside of it. He moved the royal court to the vast new palace complex he built at Versailles, southwest of the city. Louis' dislike of Paris probably stemmed from the trauma he experienced as a child during the Fronde, a brutal uprising that shook the capital. It was the Paris mob who rose up once again, this time in 1789, to storm the Bastille and spark off the French Revolution which led to the eventual overthrow of the monarchy in 1792.

Paris has been called the capital of the 19th century but militarily it didn't fare too well. Occupied by Russian Cossacks after Napoleon's defeat in 1814, it also suffered at the hands of the Prussians in 1871. Despite these humiliating setbacks, the city made a remarkable job of beautifying itself during this time, particularly during the Second Empire under Napoleon III. The Emperor's chief planner was Baron Haussmann, who transformed the capital between 1852 and 1870. Cutting wide boulevards through the medieval fabric of the city, he levelled entire districts in the process. The spider's web of avenues linking star-like clusters of streets that characterises Paris today were all laid out in this era. These were lined with uniformly elegant apartment buildings that were built out of granite and sandstone facing out over the wide pavements and broad boulevards scattered with benches, street lighting and trees. The reason for this redevelopment was in fact twofold: it of course beautified and sanitised the city, but it also facilitated troop movements in the event of any popular uprisings against the emperor.

The Second Empire came to a humiliating end when Napoleon III's forces were defeated by the Prussians in 1870–71. Paris fell on 28 January 1871 and the people, disgusted at their government's capitulation, rose up to form the Paris Commune. This uprising came to a bloody end in May 1871 when about 20,000 Communards were killed by government troops (who were well able to make use of Baron Haussmann's boulevards).

The city quickly put this trauma behind it, however, and hosted two major international expositions. One in 1889, the centenary of the French Revolution, and another in 1900. Many beautiful buildings and bridges were built to facilitate these events, including, of course, the Eiffel Tower – the world's tallest structure until 1931. This was only supposed to be temporary and was saved from demolition because of the invention of radio (it made a useful antenna).

Between the world wars, Paris became an international gathering place for some of the most famous and influential artists and writers the world has ever seen. Picasso, Dali, Hemingway and Joyce all made their home here amid the laid-back cultural milieu of the city's bars and cafés. This came to a sudden end with World War II. Paris fell to the Germans in June 1940. It remained under occupation until August of 1944. One good thing about having fallen with so little resistance was that the city was able to emerge from the war virtually unscathed and quickly regained its reputation as a cultural capital, with artists, writers and thinkers all flocking back to districts such as St-Germain on the Left Bank.

The city's suburbs spread rapidly after World War II, which may have eased pressure on space in the city centre, but led to ghettos of poverty and unease. The student riots of 1968 were followed by further uprisings in the 1980s, with outbreaks of violence flaring up occasionally ever since. Paris is still one of the world's most beautiful cities, however, as well as being wonderfully rich in culture and entertainment. A number of recent presidents, emulating the kings who preceded them, have graced the city with major architectural projects. President Mitterrand's series commemorating the 200th anniversary of the French Revolution is perhaps the most famous. His Grands Projets include the impressive Grande Arch at La Défense and the famous Pyramid of the Louvre, both startling modern interventions that show Paris is still at the forefront of world architecture as it enters the 21st century.

Note: the *flâneur*

The *flâneur* is a person who wanders aimlessly around a city. The French verb *flâner* means 'to stroll' and it was the poet Charles Baudelaire who developed the notion of the *flâneur* or a person who walks the streets of a city in order to garner experiences. Seemingly without purpose, the *flâneur* is often secretly in tune with a city's history and inner life as they go about in search of a brush with the unexpected.

Performers in piazza, Pompidou Centre

A Note on Climate

Paris in the spring – a phrase redolent of romance. Indeed, spring is one of the best times to visit the city, as it can get uncomfortably hot in summer, when anyone who can do so decamps to cooler climes. Paris has an typically oceanic climate which is mild and only moderately wet. Summers are usually warm, with temperatures averaging 15 to 25°C (60 to 80°F), but they can occasionally rise above 32°C (90°F) and have been known to hit 40°C (104°F). Spring and autumn are mild but fresh and unstable, while winter months are cold but rarely freezing. Temperatures average around 7°C (45°F) and snowfall is rare. Rain falls throughout the year, but Paris is not a particularly rainy city. It can, however, have sudden heavy showers, so be prepared.

A Note on Icons

To inform readers about some of the interesting features in the places mentioned in this book, we have added icons representing the following:

 Must See

 National Monument

 Good View

 See At Night

 Drinking

 Eating

 Shopping

Western Europe

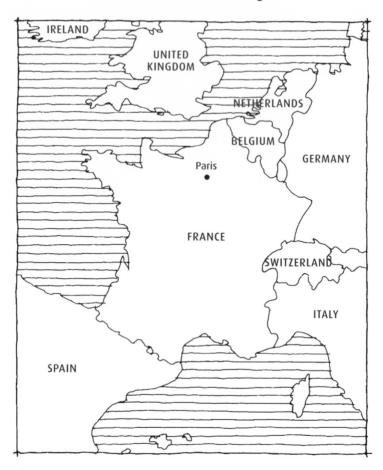

Paris Districts

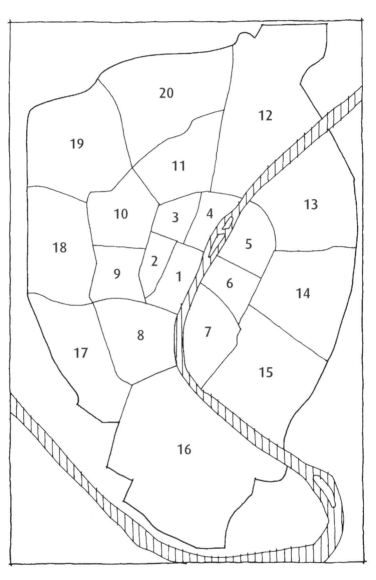

Paris: 'That lamp for lovers hung in the wood of the world.'

— James Joyce

The Islands

The Islands

This is where it all began. Paris was first inhabited by Celtic tribes over 2,000 years ago, when the Ile de la Cité was a convenient river crossing on the major north-south route through the country. In fact, it was the Parisii tribe that gave the city its name. Paris was still a small village when the Romans arrived under Julius Caesar in 53 BCE. They established a settlement here, calling it Lutetia. After the fall of Rome, the Franks and Capetian kings continued to develop the city, establishing the islands as a major centre for political and religious power. The Palais de Justice, with its former prison the Conciergerie, and the Gothic masterpieces of Notre-Dame and Sainte-Chapelle stand as testament to this colourful time in the city's history.

In the early 17th century the islands were partially redeveloped, with the building of the beautiful Pont Neuf and the laying out of Square du Vert-Galant and Place Dauphine making elegant openings in the dense medieval fabric of the city. This was further redeveloped in the 19th century, when the Parvis de Notre-Dame was cleared by Baron Haussmann to allow for a clearer view of the cathedral. Vestiges of medieval city life can still be seen in the old Marché aux Fleurs. The smaller of the two islands, Ile St-Louis, is connected to Ile de la Cité by a bridge. This charming area of elegant 17th-century residences was once a swamp, but is now an exclusive housing enclave.

THE WALK

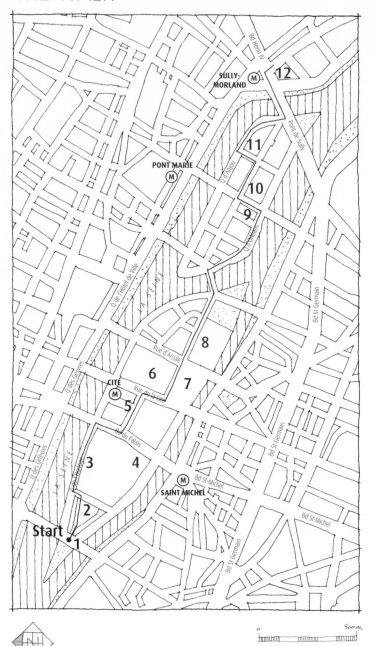

KEY

1. Pont Neuf
2. Place Dauphine
3. Conciergerie
4. Sainte-Chapelle
5. Marché aux Fleurs
6. Hôtel Dieu
7. Crypte Archéologique
8. Notre-Dame de Paris
9. Société Historique et Littéraire Polonaise
10. St-Louis-en-l'Ile
11. Hôtel de Lauzun
12. Pavillon de l'Arsenal

The Islands

The islands

Pont Neuf ❶

Leave Pont Neuf station and you will be at Pont Neuf, one of the prettiest and most famous bridges in Paris. Straddling both sides of Ile de la Cité, the Square du Vert-Galant sits at its middle, sticking out into the Seine like the prow of a ship. Despite its name (which translates as 'new bridge'), this is the oldest bridge in the city and was also for many years the widest. The foundation stone was laid by Henri III in 1578, but changes to the bridge's design as well as the vicissitudes of the Wars of Religion delayed its construction. Henri IV finally declared it open in 1607. Like most bridges of its time, it was built as a series of short-arched constructions, a model devised by the Romans.

Pont Neuf consists of 12 arches, five joining the Left Bank to the Ile de la Cité, and the other seven linking the island to the Right Bank on the other side of the Seine. The bridge is made up of two separate spans, with a total length of 275 metres (912 feet). It has been repaired and renovated many times, including changing the arches from the original almost semi-circular form to the more elliptical arches we can see today (this was done in 1848–1855). A major restoration begun in 1994 was completed in time for the bridge's 400th anniversary in 2007.

Where the two arms of the bridge meet stands a magnificent equestrian **statue of Henri IV** commissioned by Marie de Medicis, Henri's widow. Erected in 1618, it was destroyed during the Revolution and rebuilt in 1818. The small park overlooking the Seine at the back of the statue is known as **Square du Vert-Galant** and is named in honour of Henri IV, known as the 'green gallant'.

Did You Know?
Pont Neuf was the first stone bridge in Paris not to have houses built on it.

Place Dauphine ❷

Opposite the statue of Henri IV lies the entrance to Place Dauphine. This triangular-shaped square was laid out just after the Pont Neuf opened, and Henri IV named it for his heir, the Dauphin (later Louis XIII). This was one of the earliest urban planning projects in the city. The site comprising of three riverine islets was little more than mud banks when Achille du Harlay began to lay out the thirty-two houses which were all designed in the same style. The narrow western wedge of the square is flanked by two pavilions facing the Seine. Like the Place des Vosges, these houses were built of brick with limestone detailing, and their steep slate roofs contain dormer windows. One of the few buildings to have avoided any restoration is No. 14.

The eastern end of the square was demolished to allow for an unimpeded view of the **Palais de Justice**. This monumental white marble building was built between 1857 and 1868 and forms the western end of a vast complex built over the former royal palace of St Louis. Stretching the entire width of the Ile de la Cité, this block has been occupied since Roman times. Charles V moved the royal court to the Marais in the 14th century, but the buildings here are still used for their original judicial and legislative functions. This was Paris' parliament from the 16th century until the Revolution. Now it is home to the city's Court of Appeal as well as the Cour de cassation, France's highest legal jurisdiction.

Palais de Justice
Opening times: 9am–6.30pm, Mon–Fri
Tel: 01. 44 32 52 52

Pont Neuf

The Islands

Conciergerie ❸

With the Palais de Justice on your right, walk up the short rue de Harlay and turn right. The Conciergerie will be on your right along the Quai de l'Horloge (with its entrance around the corner at No. 2 Boulevard du Palais). A distinctly medieval-looking fortress, this vast building with its towers facing the Seine was once a notorious prison. During the Revolution, hundreds of prisoners were taken from here to be executed by guillotine. It actually began life as a royal palace and still forms part of the vast Palais de Justice complex.

Originally occupied by Romans, this part of the Ile de la Cité was subsequently occupied by a Merovingian palace. This was massively extended and fortified by St Louis and Philippe IV (Philip the Fair – meaning good-looking) in the 13th and 14th centuries, with Louis adding the magnificent Sainte-Chapelle around the corner. Philippe was responsible for the turreted facade overlooking the river.

The Conciergerie's Grande Salle (great hall) was one of the largest in Europe, and its lower storey, La Salle des Gens, still survives today. Meauring 64 metres (210 feet) long, 27.5 metres (90 feet) wide and 8.5 metres (28 feet) high, it used to be the dining room for the palace staff, but was also occasionally used for banquets and judicial proceedings.

Charles V abandoned the palace in 1358 when he moved the court to the Louvre, but the palace continued to serve in an administrative capacity, as home to the chancellery and the French parliament. It was converted into a prison in 1391. As was usual for the time, prisoners who could afford to do so would get a private cell and better food. Poorer people had to make do with simply furnished cells called *pistoles*, while the very poor, known as *pailleux* (from the hay or *paille* they slept on) were confined to hideous little holes called *oubliettes* where they were often forgotten about – *oubliette* literally means 'forgotten about'.

The Conciergerie gained its reputation for grimness during the Revolution, when it became known as the 'antechamber to the guillotine'. It held as many 1,200 prisoners, both male and female, at any one time. It was also home to the feared Tribunal, which sat in the Grande Salle between 1793 and 1795 and condemned a staggering 2,600 people to the guillotine, the most famous being Queen Marie-Antoinette and Charlotte Corday (the murderer of the Revolutionary leader Marat, whom she killed in his bath).

In the 19th century the Conciergerie continued to be used as a prison, but Marie-Antoinette's former cell was converted into a sort of shrine. Decommissioned as a prison in 1914, the Conciergerie is now open to the public – although only a small part of this vast complex is accessible as it is also home to the Paris law courts. Both the Conciergerie and the Palais de Justice were refurbished in the mid-19th century, which completely altered their appearance. The former may look like a brooding medieval fortress, but this only dates back to 1858 when it was 'restored' by Viollet-le-Duc.

Three towers survive from the medieval era, the Caesar Tower, the Silver Tower and the Bonbec ('good beak') Tower (which got its name from the

torture chamber where victims were encouraged to tell all they knew – or 'sing like a bird with a good beak'). The 14th-century clock on the Tour de l'Horloge is the city's oldest, and is still working.

Conciergerie

Opening times: 9.30am–6pm daily (until 5pm Nov to the end of Feb) (last admission 30 minutes before closing). Closed 1 Jan, 1 May, 25 Dec Combined ticket with Sainte-Chapelle available.
Website: www.monum.fr
Tel: 01. 53 40 60 80

Conciergerie

Sainte-Chapelle ❹

Continue along Quai de l'Horloge and turn right, the Sainte-Chapelle will be on your right after the Cour du Mai, which is the majestic main courtyard of the Palais de Justice. Built by St Louis between 1239 and 1243, this is one of the most breathtakingly beautiful buildings in the whole of France. Regarded as a high point in the Rayonnant Gothic style, the chapel's 15 magnificent stained-glass windows are separated by the slimmest of stone columns soaring 15 metres (50 feet) into the air to support the blue-painted roof that is studded with gold stars – the symbol of the Blessed Virgin.

The Islands

Built as a reliquary to house a precious religion relic – Christ's Crown of Thorns, which St Louis bought from the Holy Roman Emperor – the Crown forms a decorative motif on some of the columns' capitals. (The Crown is no longer housed here, having been moved to the treasury of Notre-Dame.) Louis probably got the idea of a chapel which could be accessed from his private quarters from the Holy Roman Emperor's palace in Constantinople, and the chapel's original entrance was located on the first floor, connecting directly to the royal apartments.

Like most Gothic buildings, there is little record about who might have designed it, although the name Pierre de Montreuil is sometimes mentioned (he completed Notre-Dame's façade). One of the chapel's highlights has to be the magnificent stained-glass windows, which portray over 1,000 religious scenes in a luxurious palette of rich religious hues. The Rose Window was installed later, as a gift from Charles VIII in 1485.

The chapel suffered badly during the Revolution, when its 75-metre (245-foot) steeple was destroyed and the relics removed. Because the Revolutionary authorities though it too dark to be used as an archive, they simply removed a lot of the glass, either selling it or letting it be destroyed. It was restored by Eugène Viollet-le-Duc from 1855 and became a national historic monument in 1862. Despite the ravages of history, nearly two-thirds of the windows are authentic.

Sainte-Chapelle
Opening times: 9.30am–6pm daily Mar–Oct; 9am–5pm daily Nov–Feb (last admission 30 minutes before closing). Closed 1 Jan, 1 May, 25 Dec Combined ticket with Conciergerie available.
Tel: 01. 53 40 60 97

> **Did You Know?**
> St Louis spent more money on the Crown of Thorns than he did on the chapel he built to house it, more than three times in fact.

Marché aux Fleurs ❺
Leave the Sainte-Chapelle by turning left back up the Boulevard du Palais and take a right onto rue de Lutèce. The Marché aux Fleurs will be on your left on Place Louis-Lépine. This charming flower market, one of the last to remain in the city centre, has been located here since 1808. This lively year-round market adds a dash of colour to an otherwise arid area of stone. Its quaint metal pavilions are home to a vast array of flowers, shrubs, plants and trees, whose seasonal colours brighten this part of the city throughout the year. On Sundays there is also a Bird Market (**Marché aux Oiseaux**) where rare breeds are for sale along with the accessories required to take care of them.

Marché aux Fleurs and Marché aux Oiseaux
Opening times: 8am–7.30pm daily

Hôtel Dieu ⑥

Continue along rue de Lutèce and the Hôtel Dieu will be straight in front of you. The main entrance is on Place du Parvis Notre-Dame, around the corner on your left. Founded in 651 by St Landry, this is considered to be the city's first hospital. It became known as the Hôtel Dieu in the Middle Ages, when it catered to the poor of the city; a tradition of charity that lasted right up until the 19th century. A large part of the building was destroyed by fire in 1772 and was not rebuilt until the reign of Napoleon. During the 19th century it was instrumental in introducing medical innovations, such as vaccination. Nuns ceased running the hospital only in 1908.

Also facing onto the Parvis Notre-Dame is the **Préfecture de Police**. The headquarters of the Paris police was the scene of intense battles against Nazi occupiers during World War II. This fact is commemorated by a plaque.

Located under the Parvis is the **Crypte Archéologique** (its entrance is in Place Jean Paul II). This is probably the most important archaeological crypt in Europe. Stretching 120 metres (393 feet) underground, it preserves the remains of buildings constructed as far back as Roman times, including traces of their sophisticated central-heating systems.

Crypte Archéologique ⑦
Opening times: 10am–6pm Tue–Sun (last admission 30 mins before closing)
Closed 1 Jan, 1 and 8 May, 1 and 11 Nov, 25 Dec
Website: www.crypte.paris.fr
Tel: 01. 55 42 50 10

Notre-Dame de Paris ⑧

Dominating the square is Notre-Dame de Paris. Famous in legend as the home of the hunchback Quasimodo, this beautiful cathedral is one of the most remarkable buildings in Paris. It is now possible to properly experience the full grandeur of its Gothic façade thanks to Baron Haussmann's clearing of the warren of Medieval streets in front of it when he created the parvis in the 19th century. The work of Maurice de Sully, and built between 1163 and 1345, it stands on the site of a Roman temple. Notre-Dame de Paris (which means Our Lady of Paris) is the seat of the Archbishop of Paris and widely regarded as one of the finest examples of French Gothic architecture.

Like many cathedrals, it took so long to complete that the fashion had changed before it was finished. This led to a substantial remodelling into the Rayonnant style in the mid-13th century. The transepts are particularly fine examples of this airy version of Gothic. The West Front contains three main doors and some good statuary, including the Kings' Gallery (featuring

BRACKEN JAN '11

28 Kings of Judah). The Rose Window depicts the Virgin for whom the cathedral is named. The North Tower contains 387 steps leading to a platform commanding wonderful views of the city, while the South Tower houses the famous Emmanuel bell. The cathedral was one of the first buildings to use the flying buttress – an arched support on the exterior that allowed a building's interior to remain column free. The spire dates from the 19th century and is by Viollet-le-Duc. It soars to a height of 90 metres (295 feet). There are two other magnificent Rose Windows, each 13 metres (43 feet) in diameter. The northern one, in the gabled portal constructed by Jean de Chelles in the 1240s, depicts Christ surrounded by saints and apostles, while the South Rose Window, in Pierre de Montreuil's southern transept dating from 1258, depicts the Virgin surrounded by figures from the Old Testament.

The cathedral's interior consists of a vaulted central nave bisected by a transept, at either end of which are the rose windows. The choir stalls were commissioned by Louis XIV (whose statue stands behind the high altar) and are noted for their exquisitely carved woodwork. The 14th-century chancel screen encloses the private place the clergy used for prayer, cut off from the noisy congregation. The Treasury, which is in the south-east corner, houses religious relics, including Christ's Crown of Thorns, which was moved here from the Sainte-Chapelle. The cathedral, like many of France's churches, was badly damaged during the Revolution, and much of its statuary destroyed. It was extensively restored by Viollet-le-Duc in the 19th century.

Notre-Dame's famous bells are rung for services and festivals. Once rung by hand, they are now powered by electric motors. The North Tower contains four bells, while the fifth and most famous, the Emmanuel, hangs in the South Tower.

Located to the rear of the cathedral is **Square Jean XXIII**. Named in honour of the pope, this pleasant little square overlooking the river was created in 1844 after rioters ransacked the archbishop's palace in 1831. A palace had stood there since the 17th century. The prefect of Paris, Rambuteau, ordered this square to be built, and the Gothic-style fountain at its heart was put in place a year after it opened. It is possible to enter the square from the cathedral via the St Stephen's door (porte St-Etienne).

Across the road from Square Jean XXIII is the **Mémorial de la Déportation**. Accessed from Square de l'Ile de France, this small triangular park juts out into the Seine. A simple memorial designed by French architect Georges-Henri Pingusson in 1962, it commemorates the 200,000 French men, women and children who were deported from Vichy France to the Nazi concentration camps in World War II. Built on the site of a former morgue, the designer's long, narrow subterranean space was intended to convey a feeling of claustrophobia. Fragments of poems by French poet Robert Desnos (a member of the French Resistance) are inscribed on the walls.

Notre-Dame de Paris
Opening times: 8am–6.45pm daily
Towers: 10am–6.30pm Apr–Sept (until 11pm Sat and Sun Jun–Aug); 10am–5.30pm Oct–Mar
Services: Mon–Sat: 8am, 9am (not in Jul and Aug), noon, 5.45pm, 6.15pm; Sun: 8.30am, 10am, 11.30am, 12.45pm, 6.30pm
Services in English: 2pm Wed, Thur and Sat
Website: www.notredamedeparis.fr
Tel: 01. 42 34 56 10

Mémorial de la Déportation
Opening times: 10am–6pm Tue–Sun
Tel: 01. 42 77 44 72

Did You Know?
The square in front of the cathedral is Point Zéro, the point from which all distances to Paris are measured.

Did You Know?
Most of the statues on Notre-Dame are not called gargoyles but grotesques. A gargoyle is a specific type of gutter spout, the rest of the cathedral's ornamentation are just imaginatively decorated statues.

The Islands

Société Historique et Littéraire Polonaise ❾

Cross the Pont St-Louis and turn right onto the Quai d'Orléans. The Société Historique et Littéraire Polonaise will be at No. 6. The romantic poet Adam Mickiewicz, who, like Chopin, lived in Paris in the 19th century, was a major figure in his native country's cultural and political life, and it is this that forms the focal point for the charming museum. Founded in 1903 by the poet's son, part of the famous Polish library moved from here to No. 74 rue Lauriston. The archives remain and form the finest collection of paintings, books, maps and emigration information about Poland outside of that country. The archive also contains some Frédéric Chopin memorabilia, including his somewhat macabre death mask.

Société Historique et Littéraire Polonaise
Opening times: 2.15–5.15pm Thur, 9am–noon Sat
Tel: 01. 55 42 83 83

St-Louis-en-l'Ile ❿

Turn left onto rue des Deux Ponts and then right onto rue St-Louis-en-l'Ile and the church of St-Louis-en-l'Ile will be on your right at No. 19 bis. The construction of this church began in 1664 and ended in 1675, but it was only consecrated in 1726. The iron clock at the entrance was installed in1741. Built to plans from the royal architect Louis Le Vau, who happened to live on the island, it replaces an earlier church dating from 1622. Its Baroque interior is richly decorated and has plenty of gilding and marble. There is also a statue of St Louis holding a crusader's sword. A 1926 plaque in the church's north aisle bears an inscription of gratitude from the citizens of St Louis, Missouri, which takes its name from the saintly French king. The church's most noticeable feature is its pierced iron spire, a remarkable architectural flourish that looks centuries ahead of its time.

St-Louis-en-l'Ile
Opening times: 9am–noon, 3pm–7pm Tue–Sat, 9am–6.30pm Sun
Closed public hols
Tel: 01. 46 34 11 60

Did You Know?
St-Louis-en-l'Ile is twinned with Carthage Cathedral in Tunisia, where St Louis is buried.

Hôtel de Lauzun ⓫

Continue along rue St-Louis-en-l'Ile and then turn left onto rue Poulletier and take a right onto Quai d'Anjou. The Hôtel de Lauzun will be at No. 17. Built by Louis Le Vau in the mid-1650s, this is one of the few *hôtels particuliers*, or

aristocratic town houses, in Paris that still contains its original interior decoration. Executed in the lavish gilt-and-mirror style of Louis XIV, Charles Le Brun is said to have had a hand in its design before moving on to work at Versailles. This pretty building has had a colourful history. It was built originally for an inn-keeper's son who had grown rich from arms dealing. Charles Gruyn des Bordes then fell foul of the king (he was closely implicated in the Fouquet affair) and was thrown into prison, where he died. His widow left the hotel to her son who then sold it to the Duc de Lauzun, who had also spent a decade in prison under Louis XIV's disfavour only to secretly marry the Duchesse de Montpensier, also known as the Grande Mademoiselle, who was able to ransom him.

Despite the whole area falling out of favour with the aristocrats in the 18th century, one of them was still living here at the time of the Revolution, the Marquis de Pimôdan. After the Revolution, the house was divided into flats and became home to a dazzling array of 19th-century luminaries, including

Hôtel de Lauzun

the poet Charles Baudelaire, who began writing *Les Fleurs du Mal* here, and Théophile Gaultier, the poet, traveller and critic. Together they formed the infamous Club des Hashischins (Hashish-Eaters' Club) to experiment with psychotropic drugs. Other famous residents included Austrian poet Rainer Maria Rilke, English artist Walter Sickert and German composer Richard Wagner. The hotel now belongs to the city and is used for receptions.

Hôtel de Lauzun
Tel: 01. 43 54 27 14

Pavillon de l'Arsenal ⓬

Continue along Quai d'Anjou. Turn left to cross the Pont de Sully and you will find yourself on Boulevard Henri IV. Take a right onto Boulevard Morland and the Pavillon de l'Arsenal will be on your right at No. 21. This is the main urban planning exhibition space in the city. Opened in 1988, it hosts regular exhibitions highlighting Paris' city planning and architecture. It also provides a forum where citizens can interact with the city authorities on issues related to planning. The Pavillon de l'Arsenal also publishes reference books on Parisians' daily life.

The building was constructed between 1878–79 and takes its name from a nearby arsenal which was built on a former Celestine monastery. Built for a wood merchant and amateur painter, Laurent-Louis Borniche, its main exhibit is a permanent display showing Paris' architecture via film, models and panoramic images. The display shows how the city has evolved over time and also highlights projects for the future. There are three other additional spaces for temporary exhibits relating to architecture.

Pavillon de l'Arsenal
Opening times: 10.30am–6.30pm Tue–Sat, 11am–7pm Sun
Closed 1 Jan, 25 Dec
Website: www.pavillon-arsenal.com
Tel: 01. 42 76 33 97

Link to the Marais walk: Return to Boulevard Henri IV and turn right, this will bring you to Place de la Bastille.

Le Marais

Nearest Metro: Bastille
Approximate walking time: 1 hour 30 minutes

Le Marais

The word marais means 'swamp' in French and this was once an area of marshes bordering the north bank of the Seine. It developed from the 14th century onwards thanks to its proximity to the Louvre. When King Charles V moved his court here, the Marais began to boom. It was the fashionable heart of Paris for centuries, until the Revolution swept away the ancient régime, a time when it was home to some of the most beautiful of the city's *hôtels particuliers*, or aristocratic town houses, many of which still exist and are open to the public as museums. In the 19th and early 20th centuries the Marias was a Jewish ghetto, but in recent decades it has begun to be fashionable once again with its chic shops and numerous excellent restaurants, bars and cafés. The area is also home to Paris' lively gay scene.

THE WALK

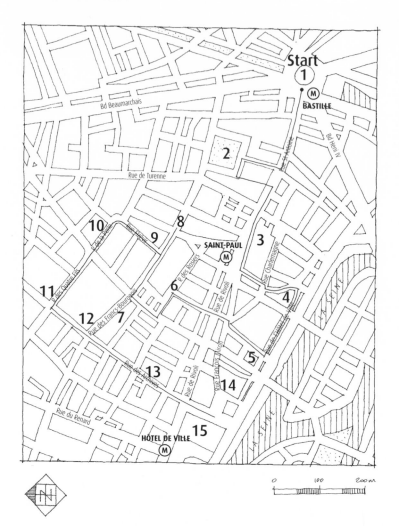

KEY

1. Place de la Bastille
2. Place des Vosges
3. St-Paul-St-Louis
4. Hôtel de Sens
5. Mémorial de la Shoah
6. Rue des Rosiers
7. Notre-Dame-des-Blancs-Manteaux
8. Rue des Francs-Bourgeois
9. Musée Coqnacq-Jay
10. Musée Picasso
11. Musée de la Chasse et de la Nature
12. National Archives
13. Cloître des Billettes
14. St-Gervais-St-Protais
15. Hôtel de Ville

Le Marais

Place de la Bastille ❶

Exit Bastille metro station onto Place de la Bastille. Nothing now remains of the celebrated prison stormed by the Paris mob on 14th July 1789, the event which sparked off the French Revolution. However, a line of stones set into the pavement from Nos. 5 to 49 Boulevard Henri IV outlines the prison's former walls and towers. At the centre of this large circus stands the imposing **Colonne de Juillet**, a memorial to those who died in the 1830 uprising that led to another overthrow of the monarchy; while the crypt below contains the remains of more than 500 victims of the 1848 revolution. This hollow bronze column soars 51.5 metres (170 feet) high and is capped by a statue known as the Genius of Liberty.

Place de la Bastille sits right on the border of the fashionable centre of Paris and the once less-than-fashionable working-class areas to the east. These have now begun to be gentrified, partly thanks to projects like the **Opéra National de Paris Bastille**. The Canadian-Uruguayan architect Carlos Ott designed this controversial 'people's opera', which opened on 14th July 1989 to celebrate the 200th anniversary of the fall of the Bastille. The massive, curved building, with its façade of glass block and granite, is far from the 19th-century tradition of opera-house design. Its main auditorium houses as many as 2,700 spectators while its performance area has five revolving stages. It also contains rehearsal areas and costume and prop workshops. The 'people's opera' idea is further reinforced by the metro station entrance and the commercial activities located in the building.

Behind the opera house is an elevated walkway that follows the old railway line that used to run to the now-vanished Gare de la Bastille. The first section is known as the **Viaduct of the Arts** and houses numerous little shops and artists' workshops. It is only nine metres wide and runs east along Avenue Daumesnil, it is an excellent way of seeing this little-visited part of the city.

Located to the south of Place de la Bastille is the **Canal St-Martin**, which links Port de Plaisance Paris Arsenal to the Bassin de la Villette in the north. La Villette is home to the elegant Neoclassical

Place de la Bastille

Rotonde de la Villette, which is beautifully floodlit at night. The canal was constructed between 1805 and 1825 to cut off a large circuitous bend in the River Seine. The stretch of canal just north of Place de la Bastille has been culverted (and is in fact the longest culvert in France), but if you follow Boulevard Richard Lenoir for about two kilometres you will come to the open section again. The canal itself is a pleasant walk, running through what was until recently a rather rundown industrial area, but which has now become fashionable, especially for nightlife. Popular with barges and pleasure boats, the canal even has a boat service, known as *vedettes*, which travels up and down it.

Opéra National de Paris Bastille
Website: www.operadeparis.fr
Tel: 01. 92 89 90 90

Did You Know?
Stones from the old Bastille prison were used in the construction of the Pont de la Concorde.

Place des Vosges ❷

Leave Place de la Bastille via rue St-Antoine and turn right onto rue de Birague. Place des Vosges will be straight ahead of you. Regarded as one of the most beautiful residential squares in the world, the 39 houses that form it are almost exactly identical and form an elegant essay in French Renaissance urban planning. Like the nearby Place Dauphine, these redbrick-and-sandstone homes were built in the early 17th century for aristocrats who wanted to be close to the royal court at the Louvre.

Designed by Baptiste Cereau, the square was originally called Place Royale and was one of the first planned squares in Europe. Begun under Henri IV, it was completed under his successor Louis XIII, and there is an equestrian statue of King Louis at the centre of the square. Started by Louis Dupat, the square was completed by Jean-Pierre Cortot after his death. Its name was changed to Place des Vosges during the Revolution. Dormer windows nestle against steeply-sloping slate roofs while the buildings' numerous balconies are decorated with ornate wrought-iron railings.

Running around the square at street level is a vaulted arcade which provides shelter. These are home to charming restaurants, cafés and shops. At the centre of the northern and southern sides of the square are larger houses known as the Pavillons du Roi and de la Reine. The square was originally a jousting venue and in 1615 saw a three-day tournament to celebrate the marriage of Louis XIII to Anne of Austria.

Cardinal Richelieu lived here for a time and the square also has a number of literary connections. The famous letter-writer Madame de Sévigné was born here in 1626, while Theophile Gautier and Alphonse Daudet both lived at

Le Marais

No. 8. No. 6 was home to Victor Hugo for 16 years. Founded as a museum in 1902 (the centenary of Hugo's birth), **Maison de Victor Hugo** commemorates the life and work of this famous French poet, dramatist and novelist who is most renowned for *The Hunchback of Notre Dame* and *Les Misérables*. From 1832 to 1848 he rented a 280-square-metre apartment on the second floor of the building formerly known as the Hôtel Rohan-Guéménée. He lived here with his wife and four children and this is also where he wrote most of *Les Misérables*. The museum contains reconstructions of his rooms, with drawings, books and mementos from his childhood right up to his exile between 1852 and 1870. It also hosts temporary exhibitions dedicated to the writer.

Leave Place des Vosges via the small door in the southwest corner and you will find yourself in the gardens of the **Hôtel de Sully** (main entrance is at No. 62 rue St-Antoine). This Renaissance-style hotel, with its pretty gardens and orangery, was built for financier Mesme Gallet between 1625 and 1630 and was designed by architect Jean Androuet du Cerceau. Gallet was a notorious gambler and is said to have lost his entire fortune in one night's gaming. He sold the hotel to the Duc de Sully in 1634. The Duc was Henri IV's chief minister, and it was he who added some of the interior decoration as well as the orangery. His grandson added a west wing in 1660, overlooking the garden. The Sully family owned the house until the 18th century after which time it passed through many different hands, suffering much damage, before becoming an historical monument in 1862 and a gradual process of restoration began. It has belonged to the state since 1944 and is an exhibition space linked to the Jeu de Paume which shows contemporary photography and film.

Place des Vosges

Maison de Victor Hugo
Opening times: 10am–6pm Tue–Sun
Closed public hols
Library: by appointment only
Website: www.musee-hugo.paris.fr
Tel: 01. 42 72 10 16

Hôtel de Sully
Opening times: Noon–7pm Tue–Fri; 10am–7pm Sat, Sun
Closed 1 Jan, 1 May, 1 and 11 Nov, 25 Dec
Website: www.jeudepaume.org
Tel: 01. 42 74 47 75

St-Paul-St-Louis ❸

Leave the Hôtel de Sully via the rue St-Antoine exit and turn right. The church of St-Paul-St-Louis will be on your left after a short distance. Located on one of the Marais' main streets, this impressive church was commissioned by the Jesuits, and the church's foundation stone was laid by Louis XIII himself in 1627. Completed in 1641, its design was influenced by the Gesu church in Rome. The neighbouring Lycée Charlemagne was originally a convent attached to the church, it became a school after the Jesuits were expelled from France in 1763. The 60-metre (180-foot) dome was a model for the later Dôme church at Les Invalides. The church was damaged during the Revolution, and most of its treasures were also removed. Delacroix's masterpiece *Christ in the Garden of Olives* can, however, still be seen near the entrance.

St-Paul-St-Louis
Opening times: 8am–8pm daily
Tel: 01. 42 72 30 32

Hôtel de Sens ❹

Continue along rue St-Antoine and veer to the left where the road splits in two. Turn left onto rue du Prévôt and then cross rue Charlemagne onto rue de Figuier and the Hôtel de Sens will be at the end on your right at No. 1. One of the few medieval buildings left in central Paris, it takes its name from the archbishops of Sens, who used to own it. It now houses the Forney fine arts library. Built between 1475 and 1507, stylistically it straddles the late Gothic and early Renaissance periods. Despite some large windows the whole building still seems to have the air of a fortified castle, which is basically what it was.

Occupied by various important aristocratic families, including the Bourbons and the Guise, it is where Cardinal de Pellevé is supposed to have died of rage when he heard that the Protestant King Henri IV had

Le Marais

Hôtel de Sens

entered Paris in 1594. Henri's wife, Marguerite de Valois, was placed here after they separated. She lived a life of debauchery not seen since the Roman empire. She is said to have had an ex-lover beheaded because he had killed her current one. The hotel overlooks a small junction. Leave this via rue de l'Hôtel de Ville and turn right. At the junction with rue de Fourcy you will be able to enjoy the best views of the hotel's lovely formal gardens.

Hôtel de Sens
Opening times: 1–7pm Tue–Sat
Closed public hols
Tel: 01. 42 78 14 60

Mémorial de la Shoah ❺

Continue along rue de l'Hôtel de Ville and turn right onto rue Geoffroy-l'Asnier. The Mémorial de la Shoah will be on your left at No. 17. This memorial to the Holocaust was opened in 2005. It consists of a stone wall etched with the names of the 76,000 Jews – 11,000 of them children – deported from France to die in Nazi concentration camps. The Holocaust Memorial Centre is home to the Contemporary Jewish Documentation Centre, which was founded by Isaac Schneerson and Leon Poliakov after the war to gather evidence of this horrific event. An eternal flame burns in the museum's crypt, in front of a memorial to an unknown Jewish martyr.

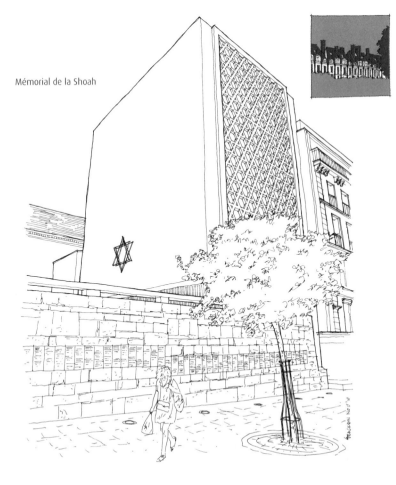

Mémorial de la Shoah

Mémorial de la Shoah
Opening times : 10am–6pm Sun–Fri (to 10pm Thur)
Website: www.memorialdelashoah.org
Tel: 01. 42 77 44 72

Rue des Rosiers ❻

Continue along rue Geoffroy-l'Asnier until you come to rue François Miron. Turn right and then immediately left onto rue Tiron. Follow this as it turns into rue des Ecouffes and you will come to rue des Rosiers. This 'street of rosebushes' smells more of pastrami and borscht these days thanks to the numerous restaurants and shops that have turned it into the heart of Paris' most famous Jewish quarter.

Known as 'the Pletzl' in Yiddish, this is one of the city's most vibrant and colourful areas. Jews first began to settle here as far back as the 13th century. There was even more immigration in the 19th century, particularly from Eastern Europe and Jews from all over North Africa began to arrive after World War II. Still home to synagogues, communal baths, bakeries and kosher shops and

Le Marais

restaurants, the area around the rue des Rosiers has also become something of a centre for fashion in recent years, with numerous stylish boutiques. It is also a popular gay hangout.

Notre-Dame-des-Blancs-Manteaux ❼

Leave rue des Rosiers by turning onto rue Vieille du Temple and you will come to rue des Blancs-Manteaux on your left. Notre-Dame-des-Blancs-Manteaux will be on the right-hand side of this street. This church was built for a mendicant order of friars and gets its rather odd-sounding name (Our Lady of the White Sheets) from the order's white habit.

Founded as a convent in 1250, the first church built here was founded by Louis IX in 1258. The present church dates from 1685, the time the monastery was renovated. The monastery was demolished during the Revolution, but the church survived. Its façade dates from another renovation, by architect Baltard in 1863, while the interior contains a wonderful 18th-century Rococo Flemish pulpit as well as a Bavarian lectern from 1749. The church's organ was designed by Kern and is quite famous. It is used in the numerous concerts of religious music the church plays host to.

Notre-Dame-des-Blancs-Manteaux
Opening times: 10am–noon, 3–7pm daily
Website: www.notre-dame-des-blancs-manteaux.org
Tel: 01. 42 72 09 37

Rue des Francs-Bourgeois ❽

Return to rue Vieille du Temple and turn left, then take a right and you will be on rue des Francs-Bourgeois. This charming street takes its name from the *francs* (free from taxes) almshouses that were built for the poor in 1334 at Nos. 34 and 36 and links rue des Archives in the east with Place des Vosges in the west. It is lined with a number of important *hôtels particuliers*, some of which are now home to museums.

The **Musée Carnavalet** is on the corner of the junction with rue de Sévigné. This is the oldest municipal museum in Paris, and also one of the largest, with more than 600,000 exhibits spread over its 100 rooms. This vast complex consists of two adjoining town houses and covers five centuries of Paris' architecture, including a series of interiors salvaged from mansions that were being destroyed. The main building is the Hôtel Carnavalet, which was built in 1548 but was transformed by François Mansart in the mid-17th century. The neighbouring mansion, the **Hôtel le Peletier de St-Fargeau**, also dates from the 17th century. The museum's collection is arranged chronologically, with the Hôtel Carnavalet covering Paris up to 1789 (with the Renaissance on the ground floor, and the 17th century up to the Revolution on the first floor), while the Hôtel le Peletier de St-Fargeau's ground floor covers the First and Second Empires. The recently restored orangery is devoted to prehistory

and the Gallo-Roman city. The idea for the museum came from Baron Haussmann. He wanted to try and preserve some of what was being destroyed as the city was rebuilt and encouraged the city council to buy the Hôtel Carnavalet in 1866 to house this new institution. Haussmann also commissioned photographer Charles Marville to record dozens of sites slated for demolition. Some of the museum's key exhibits are a Charles Le Brun ceiling from the Hôtel de la Rivière, Claude Nicolas Ledoux's gold-and-white reception room from the Hôtel d'Uzès (created 1761) and the ballroom from the Hôtel de Wendel, which is a reconstruction of an early 20th-century interior. There is also the Art Nouveau interior of the Fouquet Jewellery Boutique designed by Alphonse Mucha in 1900.

Opposite the Musée Carnavalet is the **Hôtel de Lamoignon**, with its entrance at No. 24 rue Pavée. This ornate doorway leads to a small courtyard and the rather fine mansion that is home to the historical library of the City of Paris. It was built in 1585 for the Duchesse d'Angoûleme, Diane de France, the daughter of Henri II. The building's main entrance is flanked by six tall Corinthian pilasters topped by a pediment sporting dogs' heads, bows, arrows and quivers – a reference to Diane's passion for hunting, which was also rather appropriate as the Roman goddess of hunting was called Diana. The library contains documents from the French Revolution onwards, as well as 80,000 prints showing the history of the city.

Musée Carnavalet
Opening times: 10am–6pm Tue–Sun (last admission 30 minutes before closing)
Closed public hols
Website: www.carnavalet.paris.fr
Tel: 01. 44 59 58 58

Hôtel de Lamoignon
Opening times: 1–6pm Mon–Sat
Closed public hols and 1–15 Aug
Tel: 01. 44 59 29 40

Did You Know?
The Hôtel Carnavalet was home to the famous letter-writer Madame de Sévigné for 20 years.

Musée Coqnacq-Jay ❾

Retrace your steps back up rue des Francs-Bourgeois and you will come to rue Elzévir on your right. The Musée Coqnacq-Jay will be on your right at No. 8. Also known as the Hôtel Donon, this elegant building is home to the exquisite collection of 18th-century furniture and paintings that used to belong to Ernest Cognacq and his wife, Louise Jay, founders of the La Samaritaine department store. They bequeathed their wonderful collection to the city, along with the house, a beautiful *hôtel particulier* dating back to 1575 (although its façade is 18th-century). The exhibits include paintings by Fragonard and Chardin, drawings by Watteau and Quentin de la Tour, and furniture and *objets d'art* from the period.

Musée Coqnacq-Jay
Opening times: 10am–6pm Tue–Sun
Closed public hols
Website: www.cognacq-jay.paris.fr
Tel: 01. 40 27 07 21

Musée Picasso ❿

Continue along rue Elzévir until you come to rue du Parc Royal. Turn left and follow it as it veers right and becomes the rue Thorigny. The Hôtel Salé, which is home to the Musée Picasso, will be on your left at No. 5. Pablo Picasso was a Spanish artist who spent most of his life in France. When he died in 1973 the French state inherited many of his works as a form of death duties. It decided to establish the Musée Picasso in 1985 in the Hôtel Salé, a large mansion built in 1656 for Aubert de Fontenay, who had made his fortune as a salt-tax collector (*salé* means 'salty').

Musée Picasso

This museum contains the largest collection of Picassos in the world. Currently undergoing extensive renovations, it is scheduled to re-open in 2012. Every period of Picasso's work is represented, including Blue, Pink and Cubism. Arranged in mainly chronological order, the collection starts on the first floor with the Blue and Pink periods, as well as Cubist and Neoclassical works. Exhibitions change regularly and not all paintings are on show at any given time. The ground floor also contains a sculpture garden containing Picasso's work from the late 1920s to the outbreak of World War II, as well as from the mid-1950s to the artist's death. Some of the highlights include the 1901 *Self-Portrait*, *Two Women Running on the Beach* from 1922, and *The Kiss* from 1969.

Musée Picasso
Closed for renovation until 2012
Website: www.musee-picasso.fr
Tel: 01. 42 71 25 21

Musée de la Chasse et de la Nature ⓫

Leave the Musée Picasso and turn right onto rue Thorigny and then right again onto rue de la Perle. The **Hôtel de Rohan** will be on your left at the junction with rue Vieille-du-Temple. This charming town house was built by architect Pierre-Alexis Delamair, who also designed the nearby Hôtel de Soubise at the same time. Built for Armand de Rohan-Soubise, a cardinal as well as Bishop of Strasbourg, the hotel's interior was drastically altered in the 19th century. It has been a part of the National Archives since 1927. In the courtyard, a doorway leading to the old stables features a Robert Le Lorrain sculpture of the Horses of Apollo which dates from the 18th century.

With the Hôtel de Rohan on your left, walk back up rue Vieille-du-Temple and turn left onto rue des Quatre Fils. Turn right onto rue des Archives and the **Musée de la Chasse et de la Nature** will be on your right at No. 60. Also known as the Hôtel Guénégaud, this gorgeous mansion was built for Secretary of State Henri de Guénégaud des Brosses by François Mansart in the mid-17th century. One wing of it is now home to the Musée de la Chasse et de la Nature (Museum of Hunting and Nature) which was inaugurated by André Malraux in 1967. Exhibits include a collection of hunting weapons dating from the 16th to the 19th centuries. There are also a number of hunting-related drawings and paintings including a rather fine Rubens, *Diane and her Nymphs Preparing to Hunt*, and a Rembrandt. The nature part of the museum is full of decorative artwork relating to man's relationship to his environment.

Hôtel de Rohan
Open for temporary exhibitions only
Tel: 01. 40 27 60 09

Le Marais

Musée de la Chasse et de la Nature
Opening times: 11am–6pm Tue–Sun
Closed public hols
Tel: 01. 53 01 92 40

National Archives ⑫

Leave the Musée de la Chasse et de la Nature and turn left down rue des Archives. The entire block on your left between rue des Quatre Fils and rue des Francs-Bourgeois is taken up by the National Archives, with its main entrance at No. 60 rue des Francs-Bourgeois. This is the famous Hôtel de Soubise. Centred on a huge courtyard, this beautifully symmetrical mansion was built by Pierre-Alexis Delamair for the Prince and Princess de Soubise between 1705 to 1709. Its impressive façade features twin colonnades topped by statues by Robert de Lorraine.

One of the two main buildings housing the National Archives (the other is the nearby Hôtel de Rohan), it was built on the site of an old manor house, which had been built in 1375 on the site of an older property belonging to the Knights Templar. It was the Paris residence of the ducs de Guise until François de Rohan, Prince de Soubise, bought it in 1700 (his wife, Anne de Rohan-Chabot, had been one of Louis XIV's mistresses, and he probably helped the couple pay for its construction).

The interiors, which have changed little since they were first designed by Germain Boffrand in the 1730s, are excellent examples of the ornate Rococo style. They feature work by some of the most celebrated painters of the day, including François Boucher. The *rocaille* work in the Princess's bedroom, the Oval Salon, is by Natoire and forms part of the museum of French history. Unfortunately this is only accessible to academic researchers. The building became home to the National Archives during the Revolution and Napoleon granted it to the state in 1808.

National Archives
Open for research only 9am–4.45pm Mon–Sat, phone for appointment
Tel: 01. 40 27 64 19

Cloître des Billettes ⑬

Continue along rue des Archives and you will come to the only remaining medieval cloister in Paris, the Cloître des Billettes, which will be on your left at No. 26. Built in 1427 for the Brothers of Charity, or *Billettes*, three of its four original arcades still exist. The church that adjoins the cloister is in a simple Neoclassical style. It replaced the monastery's original church in 1756.

:Cloître des Billettes

BRACKEN AUG '10

Cloître des Billettes
Opening times:
Cloister: 11am–7pm daily
Church: 6.30–8pm Thur,
9.30am–4pm Sun
Tel: 01. 42 72 37 08

St-Gervais-St-Protais ⑭

Continue along rue des Archives, crossing rue de Rivoli, and you will come to rue de Lobau. On your left is a small square, at the end of which is the magnificent church of St-Gervais-St-Protais. This beautiful place of worship is one of the oldest in Paris and is named in honour of Gervais and Protais, two Roman soldiers martyred for their Christianity by the Emperor Nero.

A Gothic church was begun here, on the site of a much older building, in the late 15th century. Its apse was finished around 1530 and the transept in 1578. The church's doorway was built by Claude Monnard between 1616 and 1620 and is in the Neoclassical style. In fact, the church is one of the first examples of this style to be found in Paris, and its façade obeys the rules of Classical architecture established by the Coliseum in Rome, consisting of three tiers of columns in Doric, Ionic and Corinthian styles. The disconnect between the Neoclassical exterior and the Gothic interior is surprising and delightful. The church also contains an excellent organ, and is where François Couperin (1668–1733) composed his two famous masses.

St-Gervais-St-Protais
Opening times: 7am–10pm daily
Tel: 01. 48 87 32 02

Le Marais

Hôtel de Ville ⑮

St-Gervais-St-Protais faces onto the rear of the Hôtel de Ville or City Hall. This ornate building is home to Paris' city council, and is a 19th-century reconstruction of the 17th-century City Hall that burnt down during the Paris Commune of 1871. Its massive bulk is elaborately decorated with carved stonework and decorative statues and overlooks a vast pedestrian square. The building is particularly impressive at night when lit up. The square was originally the city's main execution ground. It is also where King Henri IV's assassin François Ravaillac was quartered alive, with his body being ripped to pieces by four horses.

The interior of the Hôtel de Ville contains an impressive staircase as well as a huge ballroom, known as the Salle des Fêtes. Adjoining salons have decorative schemes devoted to science, literature and the arts. These are not usually open to the public but it is possible to see them during some of France's national holidays or on group visits. Certain parts of the building are also used for temporary exhibitions, usually on themes relating to France.

Hôtel de Ville
Opening times: Groups, by appointment only

Link to the Beaubourg walk: Follow rue de Rivoli away from the front of the Hôtel de Ville and turn right onto rue St-Martin.

Beaubourg

Nearest Metro: Hôtel de Ville
Approximate walking time: 1 hour

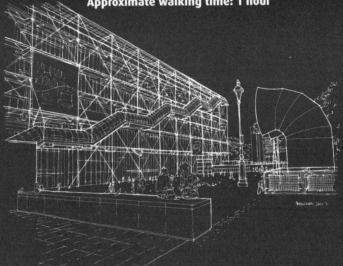

Beaubourg

This ancient part of the city is full of Gothic architecture but is actually dominated by two late 20th-century buildings: the ground-breaking Pompidou Centre and the vast Forum des Halles. The former is an industrial-looking museum that houses Paris' collection of modern art. Hulking over the quaint older buildings that surround it, the Pompidou looks like nothing so much as an oil refinery. Les Halles is a 1980s' shopping centre, most of which is underground. It replaced a wholesale fruit, vegetable and meat market knocked down in the early 1970s in an effort to improve the traffic circulation of the area. The original market buildings were beautiful and have been replaced by a shopping and leisure complex of somewhat less architectural merit, but the Forum is still a popular hangout with young shoppers, particularly those from the suburbs who can avail of the rapid rail links to this part of the city. Beaubourg is also home to some lovely churches and squares, as well as the Renaissance Fontaine des Innocents, the medieval Tour de Jean Sans Peur and the oldest house in Paris, No. 51 rue de Montmorency, which is now a restaurant.

THE WALK

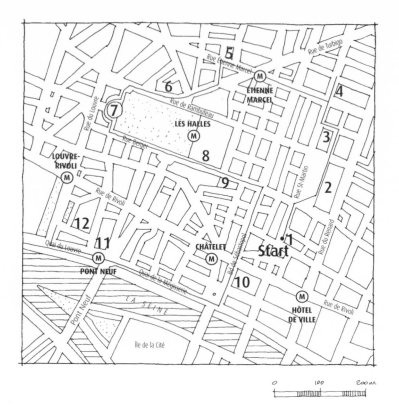

KEY

1. St-Merry
2. Pompidou Centre
3. Le Défenseur du Temps
4. No. 51 rue de Montmorency
5. Tour de Jean Sans Peur
6. St-Eustache
7. Bourse du Commerce
8. Forum des Halles
9. Fontaine des Innocents
10. Tour St-Jacques
11. La Samaritaine
12. St-Germain l'Auxerrois

Beaubourg

St-Merry ❶

Leave the Hôtel de Ville metro station onto rue de Rivoli and turn right onto rue St-Martin. St-Merry will be on your right after rue de la Verrerie. This was the parish church of the wealthy Lombard bankers, who gave their name to the nearby rue des Lombards. Built on the site of a church that dates back to the 7th century, it is named after St Médéric, the Abbot of St-Martin d'Autun, who was buried here in the early 8th century. The saint's name was eventually simplified to Merry.

This flamboyant Gothic building was not completed until 1552 and its west front is particularly decorative. The church's northwest turret contains the oldest bell in Paris, dating from 1331, while its pulpit, designed by the Stodtz brothers in the mid-18th century, sports a rather incongruous pair of carved wooden palm trees.

Continue along rue St-Martin and you will come to **Café Beaubourg** on your right. Facing onto the large piazza in front of the Pompidou Centre, this popular and stylish café was designed by Christian de Portzamparc. Created for restaurateur Gilbert Costes in 1987, its spacious terraces overlook the vast piazza in front of the Pompidou Centre as well as the smaller square across rue St-Martin. The café's double-height interior is also spacious and very elegant, it has been decorated in an understated style that is so classic and timeless that it doesn't appear to have dated at all. A popular meeting place for art dealers from the surrounding galleries, as well as Pompidou Centre staff, it serves excellent light meals and is a popular place to have a drink.

St-Merry
Opening times: 3–7pm daily
Tel: 01. 42 71 93 93

Café Beaubourg
Opening times: 8am–1am Mon–Wed, Sun; 8am–2am Thur–Sat
Tel: 01. 48 87 63 96

Pompidou Centre ❷

This is Paris' museum of modern art. It is also home to extensive reference libraries, an industrial design centre, a centre for music and acoustic research as well as administrative facilities, bookshops, restaurants, a cinema and children's activities. The building itself is perhaps even more famous than the art it contains. Designed by Italian architects Richard Rogers, Renzo Piano and Gianfranco Franchini (Peter Rice was the engineer), it completely revolutionised this part of Paris. It was also a huge influence on the course of late 20th-century architectural development. The result of a design competition, which the architects only decided to enter at the last moment, the building is influenced by Futurism, Constructivism and the Archigram collective. It was designed and built in six years, opening in 1977, and was, unusually for a structure of this size and type, not only on time but actually under budget.

It has been designed to seem inside-out. Not only is its structure expressed clearly on the exterior, but all of its mechanical and electrical functions, conduits and piping have been painted bright colours to distinguish their various functions: air-conditioning is blue, water green and electricity yellow, while the white funnels act as air ducts ventilating the building's underground areas. The architects wanted to let visitors see clearly the way a building like this functioned. The most arresting feature is the external 'people-mover', the long series of escalators that snakes its way up the front of the building, giving it a real sense of connectivity with the popular piazza outside and leading to viewing platforms that command magnificent views of the city centre.

Covering one million square feet (93,000 square metres), the Centre averages a staggering seven million visitors a year. The collections consist of over 50,000 works of art from more than 42,000 artists and represents a chronological overview of the entirety of modern and contemporary art. These include painting, sculpture, drawing and photography, as well as more recent media innovations such as cinema, visual and sound archives, in addition to architecture and design. The permanent collections are on Levels 4 and 5, with the former being home to contemporary art from the 1960s onwards, and 5 showing works from 1905 up to 1960. All the major art movements are represented, such as Fauvism, Cubism and Abstract Expressionism, and one can enjoy the works of many major artists, including Matisse, Picasso, Braque, Duchamp, Kandinsky, Léger, Miró and Giocometti. Art since 1960 features, among others, the work of Bourgeois, Basquiat and Beuys, and there is also a room dedicated to the work of French designer Philippe Starck. Levels 1 and 6 house temporary exhibitions, while Levels 1, 2 and 3 are home to an information library.

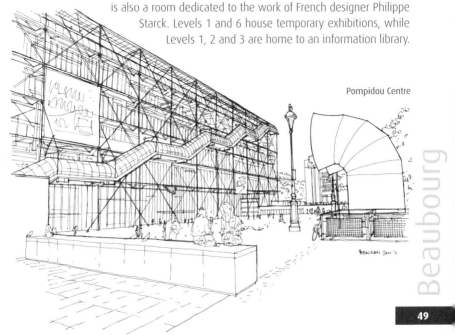

Pompidou Centre

Beaubourg

The lower levels are part of 'The Forum', a public area which includes a performance centre for dance, theatre and music, a cinema and a children's workshop. The piazza outside is a popular place to watch street performers, while on the rue Rambuteau side of the piazza there is a reconstruction of the studio of Romanian-born artist Brancusi, who lived and worked in Paris from 1904 and bequeathed his entire collection to the French state.

Pompidou Centre
Opening times: 11am–10pm Wed–Mon;
Library: noon–10pm Wed–Mon (from 11am Sat, Sun and public hols)
Atelier Brancusi: 2–6pm Wed–Mon
Website: www.centrepompidou.fr
Tel: 01. 44 78 12 33

Le Défenseur du Temps ❸
Exit the Pompidou Centre onto the piazza and turn right. This complex of modern buildings is known as the Quartier de l'Horloge (the Clock Quarter) and consists of a warren of small streets and laneways, with Le Défenseur du Temps (The Defender of Time), a public clock by Jacques Monastier, located at its heart on rue Bernard de Clairvaux. This impressive brass-and-steel timepiece is a four-metre-high (13-foot) mechanical sculpture that weighs one tonne. An intriguing sight when static, the clock is currently scheduled for renovation and thus not in working order. When it does work it is possible to see the passage of time being defended from attack by elements such as air, earth and water, which come in the shape of dragons. These creatures attack at the approach of every hour to the sound of hurricanes, earthquakes and tidal waves.

No. 51 rue de Montmorency ❹
Leave the cluster of streets around Le Défenseur du Temps out onto rue St-Martin and turn right. Rue de Montmorency will be the third street on your right. No. 51

No. 51 rue de Montmorency

is considered to be the oldest house in Paris. It was built by Nicolas Flamel in 1407, a book-keeper and alchemist famous for always keeping open house for the poor of the city. All he asked in return was that they pray for the souls of the dead. The house is a charming little building in a pinkish sandstone, the ground floor of which is elaborately carved in places, but the carvings are so old and worn that it's hard to see what they are meant to be. An inscription in Medieval French runs across the top of the ground floor. The building is home to a French restaurant today.

Tour de Jean Sans Peur ❺

Retrace your steps down rue St-Martin and turn right onto rue aux Ours which turns into rue Etienne-Marcel and the Tour de Jean Sans Peur will be on your right. This bizarre looking tower takes its ironic name (Fearless John's Tower) from the Duc Jean de Bourgogne, who had it built in the early 15th century in an effort to protect himself from the family of the Duc d'Orléans, whom he had assassinated in 1408. This 27-metre (88-foot) tower is all that remains of the Hôtel de Bourgogne, a magnificent medieval palace and the Paris residence of the important Bourgogne family. The tower housed the Duc's bedroom, which was on the fourth floor and reached by a flight of 140 steps. The magnificently decorated stone ceiling in the lower part of the tower represents leaves and branches from an oak tree, supposedly symbolising the strength and longevity of the house of Bourgogne.

Tour de Jean Sans Peur

Tour de Jean Sans Peur
Opening times: 1.30–6pm Wed, Sat and Sun, early Nov–end March; 1.30–6pm Wed–Sun, April–early Nov
Website: www.tourjeansanspeur.com
Tel: 01. 40 26 20 28

Beaubourg

St-Eustache ❻

Continue along rue Etienne-Marcel and turn left onto rue Française and then right at rue de Turbigo and you will come to St-Eustache. Like the church of St-Gervais-St-Protais, St-Eustache also began construction as a Gothic building, only to be finished in a Renaissance Neoclassical style. Despite its somewhat unfinished appearance – the Neoclassical front is missing one of its towers, it makes for a startling contrast to the rest of the Gothic building – St-Eustache has to be one of the most beautiful churches in the city. Attributed to Italian architect Domenico da Cortona, the interior is clearly modelled on Notre-Dame, with its five naves and side and radial chapels, while the front resembles St-Sulpice. The stained-glass windows in the chancel were created from cartoons by Philippe de Champaigne.

Named for St Eustace, a Roman general burnt along with the rest of his family for being Christian, the church is associated with a number of famous figures, including Molière, the Marquise de Pompadour (Louis XV's mistress) and Cardinal Richelieu, all of whom were baptised here. It is also the place Mozart chose for his mother's funeral.

Like all churches during the Revolution, St-Eustache was desecrated, although some fine paintings by Rubens are still to be seen. The church frequently hosts concerts on its magnificent organ.

St-Eustache
Opening times: 9.30am–7pm Mon–Fri; 10am–7pm Sat; 9.15am–7pm Sun
Services: 12.30pm, 6pm Mon–Fri; 6pm Sat; 9.30am, 11am, 6pm Sun
Organ recitals: 5.30pm Sun
Tel: 01. 42 36 31 05

Bourse du Commerce ❼

Diagonally across from the front of St-Eustache is the Bourse du Commerce at No. 2 rue de Viarmes. Built on the site of a series of royal town houses, architect Nicolas Le Camus de Mezieres built a circular corn exchange here between 1763 and 1767. Pierced by 25 arches, the central courtyard remained open to the elements, but two concentric galleries, which were also open, allowed for a certain amount of shelter. These were supported by Tuscan columns.

As the open courtyard affected the quality of the grain stored, a dome was built in 1782–83 by Jacques-Guillaume Legrand and Jacques Molino. This was much admired but destroyed by fire in 1802. It was rebuilt between 1806–11. The dome's iron and copper cladding were replaced by glass in 1838. Victor Hugo hated it, comparing it to a jockey's cap. Again ravaged by fire in 1854, it eventually closed down in 1873 and was turned into a Chamber of Commerce by architect Henri Blondel in 1885. He altered the dome, closed the arcades and dressed the entire building in stone. It officially opened in 1889 and was restored again in 1989. It is still home to an electronic futures market.

Bourse du Commerce
Opening times: 9am–5pm Mon–Fri
Tel: 01. 55 65 55 65

Did You Know?
The City of Paris sold the Bourse du Commerce to the Chamber of Commerce in 1949 for the sum of one franc.

Forum des Halles ❽

The Bourse du Commerce overlooks the Forum des Halles, a vast underground shopping complex with a central open-air portion located below ground level and surrounded by roof gardens with walkways, pergolas and pavilions at street level. The shops occupy two levels and contain everything from chic boutiques to megastores, as well as a multiplex cinema and a swimming pool. It is also home to the world's busiest underground station (Châtelet les Halles), linking the Paris metro to the major suburban railway (the RER).

Built in 1979, the complex is simply referred to as Les Halles. It replaced the old wholesale fruit, vegetable and meat market of the city, which was a vast iron-and-glass complex designed by Victor Baltard in the 1850s known as the 'belly of Paris'. The area had traditionally been the site of a market, dating all the way back to the 1180s when King Philipp-Auguste built a shelter for merchants to sell their wares. The wholesale market moved to Rungis on the outskirts of Paris in the 1960s and Les Halles was dismantled in 1971. Its replacement has never been popular and there are frequent discussions about ways it could be improved.

Located at No. 2 the Grande Galerie is the **Forum des Images**. This shop sells thousands of cinema, television and amateur films, many of which feature Paris. Some of the footage dates back to 1895 and includes newsreels of General de Gaulle avoiding sniper fire during the 1944 Liberation of Paris. The Forum also hosts 'Cours de Cinéma' in the evenings, where classic films are discussed.

Forum des Images
Opening times: 1–9pm Tue–Sun
Website: www.forumdesimages.net
Tel: 01. 53 01 96 96

Fontaine des Innocents ❾

Leave Forum des Halles via rue Berger and turn left. You will come to a small square at the junction of rue St-Denis. At the centre of the square sits this elegant stepped fountain. Originally called the Fountain of the Nymphs, the Fountain of the Innocents is the last Renaissance fountain left in Paris and was,

Beaubourg

Fontaine des Innocents

ironically, also the first to be built, by architect Pierre Lescot and sculptor Jean Goujon between 1547–50. Originally located on the rue St-Denis, it moved to its present position at the centre of this charming square in the 18th century. This square used to be a graveyard attached to a church called St-Innocents, hence its name. The fountain has recently been restored and is a popular place for young people to meet as it's a well-known landmark at an important crossroad in this busy part of the city.

Tour St-Jacques ⑩

Continue along rue Berger and turn right onto Boulevard de Sébastapol. The Tour St-Jacques will be on your left after the rue de Rivoli. This tower is all that remains of the 16th-century church of St-Jacques-de-la-Boucherie (St James of the Butchery), which was demolished after the French Revolution. The church's strange name comes from the fact that the wholesale butchers from the nearby Les Halles market worshipped here, and also helped to pay for its lavish late Gothic decoration.

The church had been a popular starting-off point for Parisians setting off on pilgrimage as it was on the road to Tours. Most pilgrims would follow the Route of St James, which led all the way to Sant'Iago de Compostela in Spain. A relic of St James was housed in the church. The tower was built between 1509 and 1523 and the stonemasons responsible for its magnificent decoration were Jean de Felin, Julien Ménart and Jean de Revier. It was recently renovated and reopened in 2009. There is a memorial to Blaise Pascal, the 17th-century mathematician, in the form of a statue on the ground floor. He used to conduct barometrical experiments here.

Tour St-Jacques
Tel: 06. 13 61 25 01

La Samaritaine ⑪

Continue along Boulevard de Sébastapol and you will come to a symmetrical square flanked by the Théâtre de la Ville on your left and the Théâtre du Châtalet on your right. At the centre sits the **Fontaine du Palmier**, one of a series of fountains commissioned by Napoleon to provide fresh drinking water for the citizens of Paris. It dates from 1806–08 and is the largest of those still existing. Designed by engineer François-Jean Bralle in the Empire style, the sculpted palm leaves at the top commemorate Napoleon's Egyptian campaign. The statue of Victory at the top is of gilded bronze and is by sculptor Louis-Simon Boizot. The present statue is a copy, the original having been moved to the Musée Carnavalet.

The twin theatres facing the square were commissioned by Baron Haussmann and built by architect Gabriel Davioud between 1860 and 1862. The **Théâtre du Châtalet** stands on the site of a small châtelet or fortress and seems identical to the Théâtre de la Ville opposite – in fact they both have very different interiors. Originally used for drama performances, the Théâtre du Châtalet became a popular venue for operettas in the 20th century. It is most famous for the 64-year run of its stage adaptation of Jules Verne's *Around the World in Eighty Days*, which was only stopped by the German occupation in 1940. This is also where Diaghilev's Ballet Russes made their Paris première. The **Théâtre de la Ville** burnt down during the Paris Commune in 1871 and was rebuilt identically three years later.

Beaubourg

Exit the square by turning right onto the Quai de la Mégisserie and follow it until you come to **La Samaritaine** just after Pont Neuf. This famous department store was founded in 1900 by Earnest Cognacq. It closed down in 2005, partly because the building no longer satisfied safety codes, but also because it had been operating at a loss for decades. It is due to reopen, eventually.

Cognacq opened his first shop in 1869, having started selling ties under an umbrella on Pont Neuf. He and his wife, Marie-Louise Jay, then rented a space on the rue de la Monnaie and did so well that they were able to open their own department store in 1900. This 11-storey building got an Art Nouveau makeover between 1903 and 1907 from architect Frantz Jourdain, and was radically altered again in 1933 by Henri Sauvage, this time in the fashionable Art Deco style. The store's name comes from a fountain that operated near Pont Neuf between 1609 and 1813. It had a gilded bas-relief showing a scene from St John's Gospel where a Samaritan women drew water from a well for Jesus. Cognacq and his wife were avid collectors of 18th-century art and their treasures are now housed in the Marais quarter's Musée Cognacq-Jay.

St-Germain l'Auxerrois ⓬

Following Quai du Louvre, continue along the river and turn right onto Cour Carrée. The magnificent east front of the Louvre will be on your left, and facing it overlooking a small green space is St-Germain l'Auxerrois. This was the parish church of the kings of France after the Valois court moved from the Ile de la Cité to the Louvre in the 14th century. Originally founded in the 7th century, stylistically it is a strange mix of Gothic and Renaissance, with the north tower only added in 1860. Its most arresting feature is the front porch, by Jean Gaussel, and it also has a beautiful rose window. The interior contains a wonderful carved wooden Flemish altarpiece and a churchwarden's pew, which was made from drawings by Charles Le Brun by François Le Mercier in 1683.

The church's many historical associations include the shameful starting of the St Bartholomew's Day Massacre on 24 August 1572. To the tolling of the church's bell, French Protestants, who had been lured to the city to celebrate the marriage of Catholic Margaret of Valois (the king's sister) to the Protestant Henri of Navarre, were brutally murdered. Despite suffering badly during the Revolution (when it was used as a barn), the church suffered even more at the hands of 'restorers' in the 19th century, although this charming structure still manages to retain its character as a jewel of Gothic architecture.

St-Germain l'Auxerrois
Opening times: 8am–8pm daily
Tel: 01. 42 60 13 96

Link to the Tuileries walk: Leave Cour Carrée via rue du Louvre and follow it until you come to rue Etienne-Marcel and turn left.

Tuileries

Nearest Metro: Louvre Rivoli
Approximate walking time: 2 hours

Tuileries

This area is the very heart of Paris, with the magnificent Musée du Louvre sitting as the focal point of the huge axis that runs all the way along the Champs-Elysées up to the Arc de Triomphe and beyond. The Louvre's main courtyard opens onto the beautifully landscaped Jardin des Tuileries, which in turn faces the impressive Place de la Concorde. Just to the north of the Louvre sits the Palais Royal, once a royal residence, now an elegant series of buildings arranged around a garden arcaded by shops. This nestles alongside the Comédie Française, France's most famous theatre. The district is also home to elegant streets and squares, including the rue de Rivoli and the Place Vendôme, all lined with chic hotels, restaurants and boutiques, as well as the Place des Victoires, which is centred on an imposing equestrian statue of King Louis XIV.

THE WALK

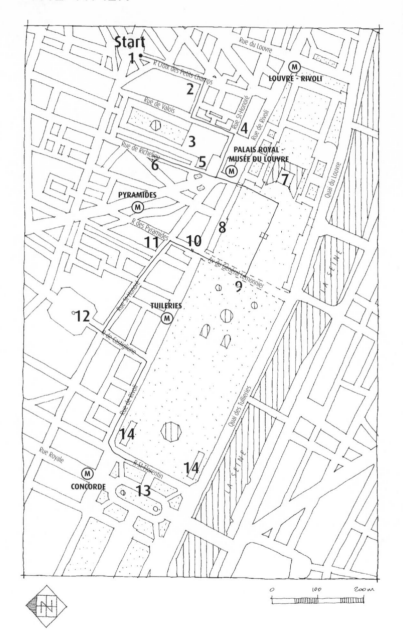

Start
1
2
Rue du Louvre
R' Croix des Petits Champs
LOUVRE - RIVOLI (M)
Rue de Valois
Rue St-Honoré
Rue de Rivoli
4
3
Rue de Richelieu
6
5
PALAIS ROYAL - MUSÉE DU LOUVRE (M)
7
PYRAMIDES (M)
R des Pyramides
8
11
10
Av du Général Lemonnier
9
LA SEINE
12
TUILERIES (M)
Rue St-Honoré
R de Castiglione
Rue de Rivoli
14
Quai des Tuileries
14
Rue Royale
R St-Florentin
CONCORDE (M)
13
LA SEINE
Quai du Louvre

N

0   100   200 m

KEY

1 Place des Victoires

2 Banque de France

3 Palais Royal

4 Louvre des Antiquaires

5 Comédie Française

6 Fontaine Molière

7 Musée du Louvre

8 Musée des Arts Décoratifs

9 Jardin des Tuileries

10 Place des Pyramides

11 St-Roch

12 Place Vendôme

13 Place de la Concorde

14 Galerie Nationale du Jeu de Paume

Tuileries

Place des Victoires ❶

Leave the Louvre Rivoli metro station and walk up rue du Louvre until you come to rue Etienne-Marcel. Turn left and Place des Victoires will be straight ahead of you. Located at the confluence of six streets, this circular public space is centred on a 12-metre-high (40-foot) statue of Louis XIV dressed as a Roman general and seated on a rearing horse. A series of private mansions were demolished to make way for this circus in the 1670s. In 1685 Jules Hardouin-Mansart designed the ring of houses that line the space today. Giant pilasters rise two storeys over arcaded bases to end in Mansart's famous two-slope roof design accommodating the dormer windows. Because the building work was incomplete at the time of the statue's unveiling in 1692, the façades of the buildings were painted onto canvas and hung as a backdrop. The original gilt-bronze statue by sculptor Martin Desjardins shows the king trampling enemies underfoot. This was destroyed precisely a century later during the Revolution, when the circus was briefly renamed Place des Victoires-Nationaux, with a wooden pyramid replacing the king's statue. This was replaced by a nude statue of one of Napoleon's generals before eventually being replaced by a new statue of Louis XIV, at the behest of Charles X in 1828. The area is extremely fashionable today and is home to some of France's most important fashion designers, including Kenzo and Thierry Mugler.

Banque de France ❷

Leave Place des Victoires via rue Croix des Petits Champs and the Banque de France will take up most of the city block to your right. France's Central Bank was founded by Napoleon in 1800 and is housed in an aristocratic town house with royal connections. The Hôtel de Toulouse, originally called Hôtel de la Vrillière, was built between 1635 and 1640 for the Marquis de la Vrillière by François Mansart. De la Vrillière was Louis XIII's Secretary of State and it was he who created the magnificent 50-metre-long (164-foot) Galerie Dorée to hang his important art collection. This has remained unchanged since it was built, although it was painted a different colour after its new owner, the Compte de Toulouse, bought it in 1712. The son of Louis XIV and Madame de Montespan, the Compte hired architect Robert de Cotte to redesign the building, which was done in collaboration with the sculptor François-Antoine Vassé. The house originally had a large garden, with a formal parterre, to the southwest. It was badly damaged during the Revolution but was restored later in the 19th century after it became the headquarters of the Banque de France in 1811. The building is now used occasionally for receptions and conferences.

Banque de France
Tel: 01. 42 92 42 92

Palais Royal ❸

Turn right off rue Croix des Petits Champs and you will be
on rue du Colonel Draint. The Palais Royal will be ahead of
you along rue de Valois. This palace, as its name suggests,
was once a royal residence. It was built, however, as the home of Cardinal
Richelieu and was originally known as the Palais Cardinal. Designed by
Jacques Lemercier, it was built between 1633 and 1639. The Cardinal left the
property to the crown after his death in 1642, when it acquired its current
name. King Louis XIII died the following year and the Palais became the
home of his widow and her two young sons (King Louis XIV and his brother
Philippe). The young King Louis nearly drowned when he fell into the Grand
Bassin while playing with some friends. He was never particularly fond of the
palace, having been holed up here throughout the terrifying Fonde, which
was one of the main reasons he chose to settle his royal court outside the
city at Versailles.

The palace passed to the cadet Orléans branch of the royal family, whose
ducs expanded the complex in the 1780s and opened the gardens and
surrounding buildings to the public where they became a sort of shopping
and entertainment complex, with cafés, bookshops and hair-dressing salons,
as well as brothels and gambling dens. The clever Duc d'Orléans survived the
horrors of the Revolution by keeping the palace gardens open to the public.
He also employed architect Victor Louis to rationalise the rear façades of the
houses that backed onto the gardens into a uniform Neoclassical whole.

Looted in the 1848 revolution, the palace passed into the hands of
the Bonaparte family and only narrowly escaped the flames of the 1871
Commune. It was restored between 1872 and 1876 and today houses
the Conseil d'Etat, the Constitutional Council and the Ministry of Culture.
The present **Jardin du Palais Royal** is about one third smaller than the
original laid out by royal gardener Peter Desgotz for Cardinal Richelieu in
the 1630s. This is due to the Duc d'Orléans' construction of the houses
on three sides of the square between 1781 and 1784. These are now
home to restaurants, galleries and shops. The garden's courtyard contains
a controversial installation by Daniel Buren. Consisting of black-and-white
striped stone columns, *Les Deux Plateaux* was installed in 1986. The houses
overlooking the gardens have some strong literary connections, with Jean
Cocteau, Colette and Jean Marais all having lived there.

Did You Know?
The Duc d'Orléans, who later became King Louis-Philippe, hired a young
Alexandre Dumas to look after his library at the Palais Royal.

Louvre des Antiquaires ❹

The bottom of rue de Valois opens onto a square called Place du Palais Royal. The Louvre des Antiquaires will be on your left. Formerly a department store called Grands Magasins du Louvres, this large three-storey building was converted into a specialist art and antique shopping centre in the 1970s. The 250 or so shops are rather expensive, so those in search of a bargain might be better off trying elsewhere.

Louvre des Antiquaires
Opening times: 11am–7pm Tue–Sun (Jul and Aug: Tue–Sat)
Closed 1 Jan, 25 Dec
Website: www.louvre-antiquaires.com
Tel: 01. 42 97 27 27

Comédie Française

Comédie Française ❺

Leave the Louvre des Antiquaires and cross Place du Palais Royal. Follow rue St-Honoré and you will almost immediately find yourself on Place Colette. France's national theatre, the Comédie Française, will be on your right. built between 1787 and 1790, this theatre has enjoyed state patronage since Louis XIV first founded a theatre company in 1680. This lovely building looks out over two pleasant, if somewhat traffic-choked, squares that are named after two writers: Colette and André Malraux. It is the setting for the works of great French dramatists such as Molière, Corneille and Racine, as well as Shakespeare and some modern playwrights. The present company can trace its roots to Molière's troupe of 17th-century actors. This understated Neoclassical building is built of a beige sandstone and is fronted by a Tuscan colonnade. It was enlarged in the early 19th century and completely rebuilt in 1900 after being damaged by fire.

Comédie Française
Tours: 9.30am, 10am, 10.30am Sat and Sun
Tel: 01. 44 58 13 16

Did You Know?
In the foyer of the Comédie Française is the armchair where Molière collapsed on stage in 1673 (ironically while performing *Le Malade Imaginaire – The Hypochondriac*).

Fontaine Molière ❻

Leave Place Colette by turning right onto rue de Richelieu and the Fontaine Molière will be at the sharp junction of rue Molière on your left. The famous playwright lived in a house on the site of what is now No. 40 rue de Richelieu. This imposing fountain dates from 1844 and replaces the earlier Fountain Richelieu which was demolished to improve traffic circulation in the area. The main statue is in bronze and was sculpted by Bernard Seuer Gabriel, while the overall design is the work of Louis Visconti, the man who also designed the fountain in front of St-Sulpice and Napoleon's tomb at Les Invalides.

Musée du Louvre ❼

Retrace your steps down rue de Richelieu and you will come to the Musée du Louvre, arguably the world's most famous museum. Few can compare in size or in the quality of its collections, which cover everything from ancient Egypt and Rome to some of the most important works of art ever created in Europe. Do not underestimate the sheer size of this museum and do not try to see everything at once. Make a list of some key items and you will invariably pass some pleasant surprises on the way. The building itself is a vast former royal palace that contains numerous courtyards and overlooks the Seine on its south side. It also acts as the focal point of the magnificent axis that runs from La Défense through the Arc de Triomphe and along the Champs-Elysées. Actually it sits a little off kilter because the axis was originally focused on the Tuileries Palace, which burnt down during the Paris Commune of 1871.

The Louvre was first constructed as a fortress by King Philippe-Auguste in 1190 to protect against Viking raids. François I then gave it a Renaissance facelift. Louis XIV and Napoleon III are mainly responsible for the building's appearance today, with one key modern exception: I. M. Pei's iconic glass pyramid which sits in the main courtyard and acts as the museum's entrance. The museum's east front contains a stately loggia of twinned fluted Corinthian columns designed by Claude Perrault, who along with Louis Le Vau worked on the Louvre in the mid-17th century. The rest of the building bears the unmistakable stamp of the mid-19th-century eclecticism of Napoleon III's

Second Empire style – Napoleon's initial letter 'N' appears in many a pediment and roundel.

Pei's pyramid dates from the 1980s and opened in time for the bicentennial of the French Revolution. First conceived in the early 1980s as a way of rationalising this vast museum, Pei's brilliantly simple design acts as a focal point for the whole complex, while its transparency does nothing to distract from the surrounding buildings. Sitting atop the Carrousel du Louvre, this visitor's complex contains galleries, cloakrooms, shops, lavatories and parking facilities all dug out of the previously underutilised courtyard. The museum's treasures date back to François I's collection – he had purchased a number of important Italian paintings, including the famous *Mona Lisa (La Gioconda)*. By the reign of Louis XIV there were still only about 200 or so works of art but donations and purchases have increased the collection steadily ever since. The museum was

Pyramide, Musée du Louvre

first opened to the public in 1793. Apart from the *Mona Lisa*, the enigmatic portrait of a Florentine noblewoman by Leonardo da Vinci, some of the collection's highlights include the *Venus de Milo*, a 2nd-century BCE statue found on Milos in Greece in 1820 and the *Marly Horses*, from the Place de la Concorde. Sculpted by Guillaume Coustou, these are the originals, replicas having replaced them at their original locations.

The museum also features European painting from 1200 to 1850, European sculpture from 1100 to 1850, Oriental, Egyptian, Greek, Etruscan and Roman antiquities as well as jewellery and *objets d'art*. The painting collections are impressive, with other works by Leonardo da Vinci as well as his compatriots Raphael, Giotto, Fra Angelico, Piero della Francesca and Uccello. The French are represented by Watteau, Fragonard, Poussin and David, while England has Gainsborough, Reynolds and Turner (France's only painting by Turner in fact). Germany's Dürer, Cranach and Holbein are here as are Spain's El Greco and Goya. The Netherlands is impressively well represented, with van Eyck, Bosch, van Dyck and Hals, not to mention Vermeer's *Lacemaker* and three Rembrandts.

Some of the highlights of the sculpture collection is *Milo of Crotona*, the statue of the Greek athlete who caught his hands in the cleft of a tree and was eaten by a lion, as well as the wild horses of Marly, which stand in the glass-roofed Cour Marly. There are also works by Duccio and Donatello as well as Michelangelo's *Slaves* and Cellini's *Fontainebleau Nymph*.

Musée du Louvre
Opening times: 9am–6pm Wed–Mon (to 10pm Wed and Fri).
Closed 1 Jan, 1 May, 11 Nov, 25 Dec
Automatic ticket booths are located in the Carrousel du Louvre
(No. 99 rue de Rivoli)
Website: www.louvre.fr
Tel: 01. 40 20 50 50

Did You Know?
I. M. Pei was the only non-French architect to be awarded one of the Grands Projets. He's a Chinese-born American and this may explain why his is the only building never to have won an award.

Musée des Arts Décoratifs ❽

Located in the northwest corner of the Palais du Louvre, this museum can be entered via No. 107 rue de Rivoli. The museum's five floors contain over 100 rooms exhibiting a fascinating collection of decorative art and design from the Middle Ages to the present day. Highlights include the Art Nouveau and Art Deco rooms as well as the doll collection. The Galerie des Bijoux is home to an amazing collection of more than 1,300 pieces of jewellery.

The adjoining **Musée de la Mode** frequently rotates its vast haute couture collections, while the **Musée de la Publicité** contains more than 40,000 posters dating between the 18th century and 1949. It also houses an impressive collection of objects linked to advertising and film. Both of these museums frequently host temporary exhibition, while the entry fee covers all three. The restaurant offers gorgeous views out over the Jardin des Tuileries.

Musée des Arts Décoratifs
Opening times: 11am–6pm Tue–Fri (until 9pm Wed and Thur),
10am–6pm Sat and Sun
Closed public hols
Website: www.lesartdecoratifs.fr
Tel: 01. 44 55 57 50

Jardin des Tuileries ❾

Lying to the west of the Louvre, these formal gardens once belonged to the Palais des Tuileries, which was burnt down during the 1871 Commune. Designed by Louis XIV's gardener, André le Nôtre, they were laid out in the 17th century and form an integral part of the landscaping that runs alongside the Seine and up the Champs-Elysées to the Arc de Triomphe and beyond.

Jardin des Tuileries

Carousel, Jardin des Tuileries

Dotted with sculptures by Coysevoix, Coustou, Sicard, Landowski and Rodin, the garden's formal lawns, trees and fountains are meticulously maintained and are popular all year round. The numerous wooden benches quickly fill up as soon as the weather turns fine enough for people to sit outside.

Located on the garden's central axis is the **Arc de Triomphe du Carrousel**, a triumphal arch built to celebrate Napoleon's victories of 1805. This part of the garden was originally known as Jardin du Carrousel and was one of the grand approaches to the Palais des Tuileries. The Arc was built by architects Percier and Fontaine in 1806–08. Its marble columns are topped by statues of soldiers from Napoleon's Grande Armée. These replace the Horses of St Mark's, which were originally placed here but had to be returned to Venice after Napoleon's defeat at Waterloo in 1815. The gilded figure of Victory at the top is by Lemot.

Jardin des Tuileries
Opening times: 7.30am–7pm (or sunset)
Tel: 01. 40 20 90 43

Place des Pyramides ⑩

Wander the Jardin des Tuileries at will and exit via Avenue du Général Lemonnier in the direction of rue des Pyramides. This small square is known as Place des Pyramides. Sculptor Emmanuel Frémiet's gilded equestrian statue of St Joan of Arc dates from the 19th century and is something of a pilgrimage site for French royalists. Joan of Arc was a national heroine who fought against the English occupation of France and was wounded nearby while fighting in 1429.

Running across Place des Pyramides is the **rue de Rivoli**. Commissioned by Napoleon in honour of his victory at Rivoli in 1797, this arcaded street is extremely long and links the Louvre to the Champs-Elysées, making it one of the most important arteries in the city centre. It is also an elegant shopping street, its arcades containing exclusive boutiques and cafés. Angélina's, at No. 226, is said to serve the best hot chocolate in town. It is also a desirable residential area, with spacious apartments housed in the elegant Neoclassical structures above the arcades, some of which were only finished in the 1850s.

Place des Pyramides

Tuileries

St-Roch ⓫

Continue along rue des Pyramides and turn left onto rue St-Honoré. St-Roch will be on your right almost immediately. This huge church is the final resting place of playwright Pierre Corneille, royal gardener André Le Nôtre and the philosopher Denis Diderot. It is also a treasure trove of religious art, much of it rescued from demolished churches and monasteries around the city. The façade still bears the scars of Napoleon's 1795 attack on royalist troops who were trying to defend it. Designed by Lemercier, the church's foundation stone was laid by Louis XIV in 1653. Construction halted in 1660, only to begin again under Jacques Hardouin-Mansart (brother to the better-known Jules) in 1701. It was he who added the Lady Chapel, which contains a lavishly decorated ceiling and dome as well as two further chapels, which expanded the church's length to an impressive 126 metres (413 feet), which is just short of Notre-Dame. Work on the church was finally completed in 1754.

St-Roch

Opening times: 8am–7pm daily
Closed non-religious public hols
Services: times vary
Tel: 01. 42 44 13 20

> **Did You Know?**
> The Marquis de Sade was married in St-Roch in 1763.

Place Vendôme ⓬

Continue along rue St-Honoré until you come to rue de Castiglione and turn right. Place Vendôme will be straight ahead of you. Originally called Place des Conquêtes (Square of Conquests) it was later renamed Place Louis le Grand (Square of Louis the Great). This stunningly elegant square was laid out in 1702 by Jules Hardouin-Mansart and forms the starting point of the chic rue de la Paix. The chamfered corners give the square a slightly octagonal feel, while the whole is space is remarkable for the sheer strictness of its symmetricality. Originally centred on a larger-than-life equestrian statue of Louis XIV, this was destroyed, as were so many others, during the Revolution, Napoleon then erected the **Vendôme column** at the centre to celebrate his victory at Austerlitz.

Modelled after Trajan's Column, 425 bas-reliefs spiral their way up the shaft. Supposedly made out of cannon confiscated from defeated enemies, the shaft's magnificent sculptures were designed by Pierre-Nolasque Bergeret and executed by a large team of craftsmen. Originally topped by a statue of Napoleon, this was pulled down after the Bourbon restoration, its metal being used to recast the statue of Henri IV on the Point Neuf. A replacement statue of Napoleon was later put back in place at the top of the column by King Louis-Philippe. The column was torn down during the Commune of 1871 but subsequently re-erected and still forms the square's main focal point today. The original plan of the square was to house academies and embassies, however, it was bankers and tax farmers who seemed better able to afford the opulent homes. The square is remarkably intact and is still home to bankers, as well as upmarket jewellers and the famous Ritz Hotel, established here at No. 15 by the renowned hotelier César Ritz at the beginning of the 20th century.

> **Did You Know?**
> Frédéric Chopin died at No. 12 Place Vendôme in 1848.

Place Vendôme

Tuileries

Place de la Concorde ⓭

Retrace your steps down rue de Castiglione until you reach rue de Rivoli and turn right. Walk along the north side of the Jardin des Tuileries and you will come to Place de la Concorde. Covering more than eight hectares (20 acres), this is one of Europe's most magnificent and historic public squares. Only two buildings actually face onto it: the twin façades of the Hôtel de la Marine and the Hôtel de Crillon. It began life as Place Louis XV, and like many another Paris square, was planned around an equestrian statue of the king (this time by Bouchardon).

Architect Jacques-Ange Gabriel designed it as an open octagon with only the north side containing buildings. The square's somewhat unusual shape may come from the fact that it was originally surrounded by a rather odd system of waterways (which have long since been filled in). Renamed Place de la Revolution during the Terror, the guillotine replaced the statue of the king, and in only two and a half years, 1,119 people were executed here, including King Louis XVI, Queen Marie-Antoinette and the revolutionary leaders Danton and Robespierre.

Renamed Place de la Concorde in an effort to erase its bloody past, the square was graced by the erection of a 3,200-year-old obelisk from Luxor in the 19th century. This is flanked by two fountains and eight statues representing French cities. The square is now the culminating point of the triumphal parades down the Champs-Elysées on Bastille Day each year.

At the northeast corner sits the **Hôtel de la Marine**. Originally known as the Gardemeuble (furniture storage), this elegant building was commissioned by Louis XV, possibly for the Dauphin. It was designed by architect Jacques-Ange Gabriel and built between 1757 and 1774. It was never really lived in, having been used as a sort of warehouse for the royal family's spare furniture. It is also where Marie-Antoinette's death warrant was signed. It has housed France's Ministry of the Marine since the Revolution. The building was profoundly altered during the Second Empire. Twinned with the Hôtel de la Marine on the other side of rue Royale is the **Hôtel de Crillon**. This is an actual hotel, and generally regarded to be one of the world's oldest luxury establishments. Containing over 100 guestrooms and 44 suites, it replaces an earlier town house, the Hôtel de Coislin. Giant colonnades rise two storeys on both buildings, in an obvious imitation of Perrault's east front of the Louvre. These form a fitting enclosure for the northern side of this impressive square.

At the southern end, across the Pont de la Concorde, sits the **Assemblée Nationale Palais-Bourbon**. Built as a palace for the Duchesse de Bourbon, the natural daughter of Louis XIV and Madame de Montespan, it was designed in 1722 by the Italian architect Lorenzo Giardini, who died within two years, so the construction was taken over by Jacques-Ange Gabriel. Completed in 1728, it initially consisted of a central block flanked by simple wings ending in symmetrical pavilions. It was then bought by Louis XV, who sold it to the Prince de Condé, a grandson of its first owner, and he got Sufflot to enlarge it. Napoleon confiscated the palace during the Revolution, then commissioned architect Bernard Poyet to build the magnificent portico in 1806 as a sort of counterpoint to the distant Madeleine beyond the Place de la Concorde to the north.

After the Bourbon restoration, the Prince de Condé rented the building to the Chamber of Deputies who then bought it outright in 1827. It has been home to France's lower house of parliament ever since. (It was also the seat of Germany's occupying government during World War II.) The adjacent Hôtel de Lassay, also built by the Prince, is now the residence of the President of the National Assembly. It is possible to enter the building and watch parliamentary debates.

Assemblée Nationale Palais-Bourbon
Opening times: Groups only, call for information
Website: www.assemblee-nationale.fr
Tel: 01. 40 63 60 00

Did You Know?
France's crown jewels were stolen from the Hôtel de la Marine in 1792. Some of them have never been recovered.

Galerie Nationale du ⑭
Jeu de Paume

Overlooking the eastern side of Place de la Concorde sit two famous galleries: the Galerie Nationale du Jeu de Paume and the Musée de l'Orangerie. The Jeu de Paume – which means 'real tennis court' – was built by Napoleon III in 1851. Real (royal) tennis has long since been replaced in popularity by lawn tennis, and this former tennis court is used to exhibit artworks. Originally famous for its magnificent collection of Impressionist art, this moved across the river to the Musée d'Orsay in 1986. The Jeu de Paume is now home to the Centre National de la Photographie, which shows exhibitions of contemporary art. It is also affiliated to the Hôtel de Sully in the Marais, which acts as an ancillary exhibition space.

The **Musée de l'Orangerie** is a lovely space and contains some impressive artwork, including the Walter-Guillaume collection, the highlights of which include some of the Ecole de Paris late Impressionist works that were created between the end of the 19th century and the outbreak of World War II. The collection includes 14 works by Cézanne and 27 by Renoir. There are also some early Picassos, and works by Rousseau, Matisse and Modigliani. The highlight of the collection is probably Claude Monet's delightful *Nymphéas* (water lily) series. Painted in his garden at Giverny near Paris, these magnificent works were presented to the French state in 1927.

Tuileries

Galerie Nationale du Jeu de Paume
Opening times: Noon–7pm Tue–Sun (until 9pm Tue), 10am–7pm Sat and Sun
Closed 1 Jan, 1 May, 25 Dec
Website: www.jeudepaume.org
Tel: 01. 47 03 12 50

Musée de l'Orangerie
Opening times: 9am–12.30pm Wed–Mon (groups only); 12.30–7pm Wed–Mon
(until 9pm Fri)
Website: www.musee-orangerie.fr
Tel: 01. 44 77 80 07

*Link to the St-Germain-des-Prés walk: Leave the Jardin des Tuileries and cross
the Seine via the bridge known as the Passerelle Léopold-Sédar Senghor.*

St-Germain-des-Prés

Nearest Metro: Solferino
Approximate walking time: 1 hour 30 minutes

St-Germain-des-Prés

An important extension to the city in the 17th century, this area is also known as the Left Bank. It takes this from its geographical location, but the word Left is also a not inappropriate one given the political views of the artists and thinkers who made the district famous. The glory days of American jazz, intellectual angst and existentialism may have gone – replaced by haute-bourgeois city life – but the places the musicians and philosophers used to hang out in the first half of the 20th century are still here, particularly the cafés lining the Boulevard St-Germain. This famous boulevard is also home to any number of exclusive boutiques, while the streets off it are a treasure trove of antiquarian books, antiques and art. On the south side of the Boulevard St-Germain are a number of quaint streets, home to good restaurants and interesting shops, as well as at the famous Odéon theatre. This area is also home to the magnificent Musée d'Orsay, a mecca for Impressionist art lovers housed in a former railway station which is a work of art in itself.

THE WALK

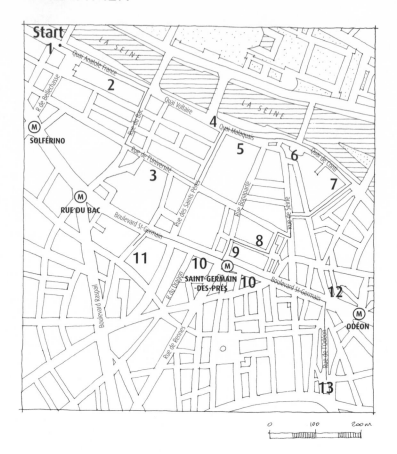

Start
1.
Quai Anatole France
LA SEINE
2
P. de Bellechasse
Quai Voltaire
4
Quai Malaquais
LA SEINE
M
SOLFÉRINO
5
6
Quai de Conti
7
Rue du Bac
Rue de l'Université
3
Rue des Saints Pères
Rue Bonaparte
Rue de Seine
M
RUE DU BAC
Boulevard St-Germain
8
11
10
9
M
SAINT-GERMAIN
-DES-PRÉS
Rue du Dragon
10
Boulevard St-Germain
12
Boulevard Raspail
M
ODÉON
Rue de Rennes
Rue de l'Odéon
13

0   100   200 m

KEY

1. Musée Nationale de la Légion d'Honneur
2. Musée d'Orsay
3. Ecole Nationale d'Administration
4. Quai Voltaire
5. Ecole Nationale Supérieure des Beaux-Arts
6. Institut de France
7. Musée de la Monnaie
8. Musée Eugène Delacroix
9. St-Germain-des-Prés
10. Boulevard St-Germain
11. Maison de Verre
12. Cour de Rohan
13. Odéon Théâtre de l'Europe

St Germain des Prés

Musée Nationale de la Légion d'Honneur

Musée Nationale de la ❶ Légion d'Honneur

Exit the Solferino metro station and walk up rue de Bellechasse until you come
to the River Seine. The Musée Nationale de la Légion d'Honneur will be on your
left overlooking the river. This museum is dedicated to the Legion of Honour,
a decoration established by Napoleon and one of France's highest honours.
The museum displays medals, insignia and paintings, as well as Napoleon's
own Legion of Honour, with his sword and breastplate. It also highlights similar
decorations from other countries, including the British Victoria Cross and American
Purple Heart. This fascinating museum is housed in the Hôtel de Salm, one of the
last of the great aristocratic town houses built before the Revolution. Its owner, a
German aristocrat called the Prince de Salm-Kyrbourg, was guillotined in 1794.

Musée Nationale de la Légion d'Honneur
Opening times: 1–6pm Wed–Sun
Website: www.legiondhonneur.fr
Tel: 01. 40 62 84 25

Musée d'Orsay ❷

The entrance to the massive Musée d'Orsay is on the parvis or small square beside the Musée Nationale de la Légion d'Honneur. Victor Laloux designed this train station and hotel for the Universal Exposition in 1900, when it was the Paris terminus of the Orléans-Paris line. Designed in 1896–97, it was built between 1898 and 1900 and uses stone from the Charent and Poitou regions. Consisting of seven impressive arches opening onto the riverfront, it contains a magnificent multi-domed vestibule which hints at Labrouste's Bibliothèque Nationale. One of three major structures built for the 1900 Exposition, the other two are the nearby Grand and Petit Palais. The building narrowly avoided demolition in the 1970s, but following an outcry from Parisians still smarting from the loss of Baltard's beautiful pavilions at Les Halles, it survived.

After 47 years of lying empty, the building was converted into a museum in 1986. This was done by ACT architecture group, Renaud Bardon, Pierre Colboc and Jean-Paul Philippon, with the Italian Gae Aulenti overseeing the interior. During the conversion a lot of the building's original features were retained.

The museum presents works of art in various media from the period 1848 to 1914. It also frames them within the context of society at that time. Occupying three levels, the collection's ground-floor exhibits work from the mid- to late 19th century, the middle features Art Nouveau decorative arts as well as a range of painting and sculpture from the second half of the 19th to the early 20th century, while the upper level contains a breathtaking collection of Impressionist and Neo-impressionist art. Many of these works came from the Louvre, while the Impressionists came from a much too cramped Jeu de Paume.

The Art Nouveau collections feature the work of Hector Guimard, the architect responsible for Paris' iconic metro station entrances, as well as Belgian architect and designer Victor Horta, the Viennese Otto Wagner, Koloman Moser, Josef Hoffmann and the Glasgow School's Charles Rennie Mackintosh, as well as American Frank Lloyd Wright. There is also some of René Lalique's jewellery and glassware. Sculpture is represented by Eugène Guillaume, François Rude and Jean-Baptiste Carpeaux, as well as Alexandre Falguière, Hyppolyte Moulin, Edgar Degas, Antoine Bourdelle, Aristide Maillol and, of course, Rodin. Paintings up to 1870 include Delacroix's *Lion Hunt* and Ingres' *The Spring* as well as Manet's provocative *Le Déjuner sur l'Herbe*. The Impressionist paintings are what the museum is most famous for, and the movement is well represented with Monet, Renoir, Pissarro, Sisley, Degas, Cézanne and van Gogh, while the Neo-impressionists are represented by Seurat, Signac, Gauguin and Odilon Redon as well as Henri (Douanier) Rousseau.

St Germain des Prés

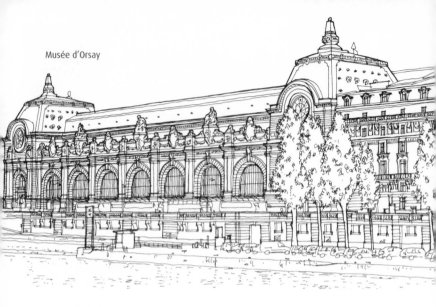

Musée d'Orsay

Musée d'Orsay

Opening times: 9.30am–6pm Tue–Sun (to 9.45pm Thur), last ticket sold one
hour before closing, combined ticket with Musée Rodin also available
Closed 1 Jan, 1 May, 25 Dec
Website: www.musee-orsay.fr
Tel: 01. 40 49 48 14

Ecole Nationale d'Administration ❸

Keeping the Musée d'Orsay to your right, walk along the river and turn right
onto rue du Bac. Then take a left onto rue de l'Université and the Ecole
Nationale d'Administration will be on your right at No. 12. Until recently
this fine building was home to the famous Ecole Nationale d'Administration,
which has since moved to Strasbourg. This is where many of France's political,
economic and scientific elite were educated.

Originally built as two houses by architect Briçonnet in the 1640s, this
elegant mansion dates from 1713 and was built by Thomas Gobert for the
widow of Denis Feydeau de Brou. She left it to her son, Paul-Espirit Feydeau de
Brou, who lived in it until his death in 1767. It then became the home of the
Venetian ambassador. It was used as a munitions depot during the Revolution.

Ecole Nationale d'Administration

Tel: 01. 49 26 45 45

Quai Voltaire ❹

Continue along rue de l'Université and turn left onto rue des Saints Pères and
you will emerge at the river where Quai Voltaire meets Quai Malaquais. This
beautiful stretch of riverfront was originally part of Quai Malaquais, it then

Apartment building, Quai de la Monnaie

became known as the Quai des Théatins before settling on the name it has today. Now home to some of the most important antique dealers in the city, it is equally famous for some of its illustrious past residents.

The sculptor James Pradier lived at No. 1. Not so well known today, even though his work is beautiful, he was highly praised and very popular in the 19th century. He is perhaps more famous now as the husband of the woman said to have swum naked across the Seine. Louise de Kéroualle also lived here, at Nos. 3–5. She was a spy for Louis XIV and was granted the title Duchess of Portsmouth by Charles II of England, who was besotted with her. No. 19 was home to composers Richard Wagner and Jean Sibelius, as well as the novelist Charles Baudelaire and an exiled Oscar Wilde. Voltaire died at the Hôtel de la Villette, No. 27.

Did You Know?

When Voltaire died, the local church (which was St-Sulpice) refused to bury him on the grounds that he had been an atheist. His body had to be rushed out of the city to avoid being buried in a pauper's grave.

Ecole Nationale Supérieure des ❺ Beaux-Arts

Continue along Quai Malaquais and you will come to the Ecole Nationale Supérieure des Beaux-Arts. This national academy for painting and sculpture was established by Cardinal Mazarin in 1648 and is still the main school for fine arts in France today. Some of the most famous artists in Europe have trained here, including Fragonard, Delacroix, Ingres, Monet, Renoir, Seurat and Sisley. It has had a huge influence worldwide, particularly in the late 19th and early 20th centuries thanks to the many American architects who studied here.

Originally located in the Louvre, the school moved to its present location at the beginning of the 19th century. It is housed in a number of buildings, the most imposing being the 19th-century Palais des Etudes, which overlooks the river from the corner of the fashionable rue Bonaparte. Designed in the Italian Renaissance style by Félix-Jacques Dubin, he received the commission in 1830 and continued working on the buildings until 1861. Dubin was a pupil of Percier, who had designed the Carousel in the Jardin des Tuileries.

The main building has a subtly decorated façade and contains numerous references to ancient and Renaissance buildings, particularly in Rome. These include triumphal arches, the Colosseum and the Cancelleria. The courtyard in front of the building incorporates an eclectic mix of medieval and Renaissance artefacts which were rescued from demolished buildings by Alexandre Lenoir in 1795, which he had originally planned to incorporate in a Musée des Monuments Français.

Ecole Nationale Supérieure des Beaux-Arts
Opening times: Mon pm groups by appointment only
Website: www.ensba.fr
Tel: 01. 47 03 50 74

Did You Know?
Rodin applied three times for entry to the Ecole Nationale Supérieure des Beaux-Arts and was repeatedly refused.

Institut de France ❻

Further along the river you will come to the Institut de France, whose central dome and sweeping wings sit on axis with the Pont des Arts. Now home to the illustrious Académie Française, along with four other institutions, the Académie is charged with compiling the official dictionary of the French language. Founded by Cardinal Richelieu in 1635, its membership is strictly limited to 40 members at any one time. This imposing Baroque building was built by Louis Le Vau as a palace in 1688 and given to the Institut de France in 1805. The impressive cupola was designed to harmonise with the Louvre across the river.

Aligned with this dome is the **Pont des Arts**, linking this side of the river to the Louvre. Built between 1802 and 1804 by the engineers Louis-Alexandre de Cessart and Jacques Dillon, it was the first metal bridge in Paris. Originally consisting of nine arches, it was built for pedestrians and was initially supposed to resemble a garden with trees, flowers and benches. Badly damaged by aerial bombardment during both World Wars, the bridge was closed in 1977. A barge rammed into it in 1979, causing a 60-metre (200-foot) section to collapse. It was rebuilt between 1981 and 1984 by Louis Arretche, who reduced the number of arches to seven, which allowed it to seem like the old one, but be aligned to the nearby Pont Neuf. Sometimes used as an outdoor exhibition space, the bridge is popular with artists who never seem to tire of painting it, or painting on it. It is also a hugely popular picnic spot, especially in summer with romantic young couples visiting Paris.

Institut de France
Opening times: Sat and Sun by appointment only
Website: www.institut-de-france.fr
Tel: 01. 44 41 44 41

Musée de la Monnaie ❼

Continue along the river and you will come to the Musée de la Monnaie at No. 11 Quai de Conti. This building, unusual for its day, was the result of an architectural competition. When Louis XV decided to rehouse the Mint he came up with this novel idea, one that has since caught on in a big way for major international commissions. The Hôtel des Monnaies was designed by architect Jacques Antoine and was completed in 1777. (The architect lived in the building up until his death.) Coins were minted here as late as 1973, at which time the process moved to Pessac in the Gironde.

The minting and milling halls are now home to a coin and medallion museum. The museum's interesting collection is displayed in a series of vertical glass display cases that allow both sides of the coins to be seen. The museum's last room illustrates how a coin's production cycle is completed and includes displays of late 19th- and early 20th-century machines and tools. While no longer a coin mint, the building still makes commemorative medallions, some of which are on sale in the shop.

Musée de la Monnaie
Opening times: 11am–5.30pm Tue–Fri, noon–5.30pm Sat and Sun
Website: www.monnaiedeparis.fr
Tel: 01. 40 46 56 66

Musée Eugène Delacroix

Musée Eugène Delacroix 8

Turn right onto rue Guénégaud and then left onto rue de Seine and right again onto rue Jacob. Then take a left onto rue de Fürstenburg and the Musée Eugène Delacroix will be on your right at No. 6. This tiny little square is popularly known as **Place de Fürstenburg**. Charming, with its old-fashioned street lamps and shady tress, it is often used as a film set. Delacroix set up his studio here when he was working on the murals for the Chapel of the Holy Angels in nearby St-Sulpice in 1857, and he continued to live and work here until his death six years later. Not only did he create the wonderful *Jacob Wrestling* for St Sulpice, he also painted *The Entombment of Christ* and *The Way to Calvary*, both of which hang in the museum. The first-floor apartment also contains a portrait of George Sand, a number of self-portraits, as well as studies for planned works. Along with the garden studio, this building is home to regular exhibitions on the artist's work.

Musée Eugène Delacroix

Opening times: 9.30am–5pm Wed–Mon (last admission 4.30pm)
Website: www.musee-delacroix.fr
Tel: 01. 44 41 86 50

St-Germain-des-Prés 9

Continue to the end of rue de Fürstenburg and the **Palais Abbatial** of St-Germain-des-Prés will be straight ahead of you at Nos. 1-5 rue de l'Abbaye. This brick-and-stone building was the residence of the abbots of St-Germain-des-Prés from the 16th century until the Revolution. Built in 1586 for Charles de

Bourbon, the Cardinal-Abbot of St-Germain and, very briefly, King of France, it was home to ten more abbots before the Revolution, when the building was sold. James Pradier, the 19th-century sculptor, had a studio here.

With the Palais Abbatial on your left, walk down rue de l'Abbaye to the end and you will come to the church of **St-Germain-des-Prés**. Overlooking the small square, this is the oldest church in Paris. King Childebert built a basilica here to house sacred relics in 542, and it grew into an important and powerful Benedictine abbey, before eventually being suppressed during the Revolution. The Revolution was not a good time to be in a religious order in France: 318 priests were hacked to death by an angry mob in a nearby monastery in September 1792 and most of this abbey's buildings were destroyed by fire in 1794. This present church dates from the 11th century but was heavily restored after the ravages of the Revolution. One of its three original towers did survive, however, and is regarded as one of the oldest belfries in France. The interior is an eclectic mix of architectural styles, with everything from 6th-century marble columns, to Romanesque arches and Gothic vaulting. It is also home to some interesting tombs, including that of René Descartes, the poet Nicolas Boileau and a King of Poland, John Casimir, who was Abbot of St-Germain-des-Prés in 1669.

St-Germain-des-Prés
Opening times: 8am–7pm daily
Services: 12.15pm, 7pm Mon–Fri, 12.15 pm, 7pm Sun
Concerts: 8pm Tue and Thurs
Tel: 01. 55 42 81 33

Boulevard St-Germain ⓿

This is one of Paris' most famous streets – lined with cafés, boutiques and bookshops, it stretches all the way from Pont de la Concorde to Ile St-Louis. Its three-kilometre (two-mile) length was the scene of the city's artistic and intellectual life for most of the 20th century. The architectural look of the street is quite uniform thanks to the fact that it was one of Baron Haussmann's great boulevards. Starting in the Latin Quarter, it runs west past President Mitterand's town house (in the rue de Bièvre), the Musée de Cluny and the Sorbonne. It is home to some of the city's most exclusive shops and restaurants, including the lavish new **Ralph Lauren** store at No. 173, which is housed in a beautifully restored 17th-century mansion. The courtyard has a charming open-air restaurant.

The boulevard's most famous restaurant is probably **Brasserie Lipp** at No. 151. Originally opened by a refugee from Alsace after the Franco-Prussian War of 1870–71 (when that part of France became a province of Germany), it is famous for its beer, sauerkraut and sausages and is popular with politicians. Regarded as the quintessentially Parisian brasserie, its interior is decorated with bright ceramic tiles sporting parrots and other fowl. Two of the most famous cafés in the entire city sit side by side: **Les Deux Magots** is at No. 6 Place St-Germain-des-Prés, while the **Café de Flore** is at No. 172 Boulevard St-Germain. Les Deux Magots takes its name comes from the two wooden statues of Chinese commercial agents, known as *magots*, that adorn one of its pillars. The café still trades on its reputation as the meeting place of the city's literary and intellectual elite. It was the favourite of artists and writers in the 1920s, including luminaries such as Ernest Hemingway who could be seen writing on its terrace. The café then became the heart of the fashionable existentialist philosophy movement in the 1950s. Café de Flore was another intellectual hangout in the 1950s, and its lovely Art Deco interior has changed little since that time. This is where Jean-Paul Sartre and Simone de Beauvoir held court.

Ralph Lauren
Tel: 01. 44 77 77 00
Restaurant:
Tel: 01. 44 77 76 00

Brasserie Lipp
Opening times: 11.45am–2am daily
Website: www.brasserie-lipp.fr
Tel: 01. 45 48 72 93

Les Deux Magots
Opening times: 7.30am–1am daily
Closed one week in Jan
Website: www.lesdeuxmagots.com
Tel: 01. 45 48 55 25

Café de Flore
Opening times: 7.30am–1.30am daily
Website: www.cafe-de-flore.com
Tel: 01. 45 48 55 26

Maison de Verre ⓫

Just off the Boulevard St-Germain is **rue du Dragon**. This charming little street dates from the Middle Ages and has a number of rather fine houses from the 17th and 18th centuries. Novelist Victor Hugo rented an attic here at No. 30 when he was a struggling young writer. Continue along Boulevard St-Germain and you will come to rue St-Guillaume on your left. **Maison de Verre** (the House of Glass) will be on your left at No. 31. Built by Pierre Chareau for Jean Dalsace and his wife Anna Bernheim, they established an influential salon here, which was frequented by intellectuals such as Walter Benjamin, as well as artists and poets like Ernst, Léger, Delaunay, Jacob and Cocteau.

Chareau managed to turn an unpromising site into a stunning Modernist house and workplace (Dalsace was a gynaecologist). Built between 1928 and 1932, this project made Chareau famous. Unlike other Modernist villas, which were invariably built on more spacious suburban sites, Chareau had a lot to contend with for this design. Not only was the plot of land restrictive, he also had to design around the top-floor tenant – who refused to move during the reconstruction – and was obliged to demolish the bottom three floors without disturbing the original top floor.

The primary materials were steel, glass and glass block, and by collaborating with Dutch architect Bernard Bijvoet and Louis Dalbet, a craftsman metalworker, Chareau reshaped the inner spaces into a warm and liveable series of volumes distributed around a massive void that is bathed in a dim light. The glass wall, until then a purely technical device, allows daylight to softly filter into the heart of the house, while the internal spatial divisions can be altered by the use of sliding, folding or rotating screens in glass or metal. The house is beautifully maintained by an American architectural historian.

Maison de Verre
Opening times: 7am–7pm daily
Tel: 01. 45 44 91 21

Cour de Rohan ⓬

Retrace your steps back along Boulevard St-Germain until you come to rue de Montfaucon on your right. The **Marché St-Germain** is at the top of this short street. Located on the site of a former fairground, this covered food market takes up the entire block between rue Mabillon and rue Felibien and was first opened in 1818. Return to Boulevard St-Germain and turn right.

Turn left onto rue l'Ancienne-Comédie and the restaurant **Le Procope** will be on your right at No. 13. Founded by a Sicilian called Francesco Procopio dei Coltelli in 1686, this is reputed to be the world's oldest coffee house. It was popular with Paris' political and literary elite, including the philosopher Voltaire, who is supposed to have drunk 40 cups of his favourite mixture of coffee and hot chocolate every day. The young Napoleon also used to come here, and would leave his hat as security while he went to search for money to pay his bill. It was also popular with the actors from the Comédie Française, which used to be located nearby. Now a restaurant, it was revamped in an 18th-century style in 1989.

The warren of ancient laneways behind rue l'Ancienne-Comédie contain a number of interesting old courtyards. **Cour du Commerce St-André** is a charming vestige of medieval Paris, although No. 9 has a gruesome association as it was here that Dr Guillotin perfected his 'philanthropic decapitating machine', the guillotine. Access to the **Cour de Rohan** is from the Boulevard St-Germain and rue du Jardinet. This is a series of three courtyards overlooked

St Germain des Prés

Cour de Rohan

by delightful old buildings housing shops and restaurants. Originally part of the 15th-century palace of the archbishops of Rouen – hence the name, which is a corruption of the original – it was threatened with demolition in 1959 but protests by concerned neighbours saved it. Henri II's mistress Diane de Poitiers lived here, and the composer Saint-Saëns was born in the rue du Jardinet in 1835. The middle courtyard is the most unusual and still retains a three-legged wrought-iron mounting block, known as a *pas-de-mule*, which was used by the elderly and the overweight when they had to mount a horse (or mule).

Le Procope
Opening times: Noon–1am daily
Website: www.procope.com
Tel: 01. 40 46 79 00

Did You Know?
Although the guillotine takes its name from its designer, Dr Guillotin, it was first used in 1792 at the behest of Dr Louis, and was known as a Louisette.

Odéon Théâtre de l'Europe ⓭

Wander the courtyards at will before returning to rue l'Ancienne-Comédie and turn left. Cross Boulevard St-Germain and you will be on **rue de l'Odéon**. Opened in 1779 to improve access to the Odéon theatre, this was the first street in Paris to have pavements with gutters. It is still an attractive and fashionable street and is famous for some of its shops, including the original location of Shakespeare & Company, Sylvia Beach's famous bookshop which stood at No. 12 from 1921 to 1940 (it is now located at No. 37 rue de la Bûcherie in the Latin Quarter). Beach was an influential figure in the literary world of the inter-war period, befriending many a struggling young writer, including Ezra Pound, T. S. Eliot, Scott Fitzgerald and Ernest Hemingway. She was also largely responsible for the publication of James Joyce's *Ulysses* (thanks to acting as a secretary, editor, agent and financier to the impecunious Irish writer).

Opposite No. 12 is *Les Amis des Livres* at No. 7. Founded by Adrianne Monnier, this famous French bookshop was frequented by the likes of André Gide and Paul Valéry. At the top of the street sits the **Odéon Théâtre de l'Europe**. This stark, almost forbidding façade was designed by Marie-Joseph Peyre. Regarded as the most influential architect in 18th-century French Neoclassicism after Sufflot, he is now all but forgotten, apart from this theatre, which was built between 1767 and 1782. Built on the grounds of the former Hôtel de Condé, the site was purchased by the king to house the Comédie Française. It was here that Beaumarchais premiered *The Marriage of Figaro*

St Germain des Prés

in 1784. The name of the theatre was changed to Odéon with the arrival of a new company in 1797. The building was destroyed by a fire in 1807 and rebuilt later that year in its original design by the architect Jean-François Chalgrin. The auditorium is a particularly impressive one, and contains a ceiling that was painted by André Masson in 1965. After World War II the theatre specialised in modern drama and was one of the best attended in Paris. Today, it hosts foreign-languages plays, including English ones.

Odéon Théâtre de l'Europe
Website: www.theatre-odeon.fr
Tel: 01. 44 85 40 40

Link to the Latin Quarter walk: Walk down rue Racine until you come to the Boulevard St-Michel.

Latin Quarter

Nearest Metro: Cluny La Sorbonne
Approximate walking time: 1 hour

Latin Quarter

This part of Paris takes its name from the fact that it was the centre of the city's education with institutes like the Sorbonne, whose students studied and spoke in Latin – the Medieval world's equivalent of English. The scene of the famous student riots of 1968, the area's proud and ancient history of learning stretches back 800 years and can be felt in the winding cobbled streets that stretch down to the river from the great university colleges and *lycées* which have been educating the French and international elite for centuries. The area has long been associated with artists and intellectuals, although these have been replaced by tourists thronging the cheap shops and fast-food outlets that have increasingly made their home here in recent years.

THE WALK

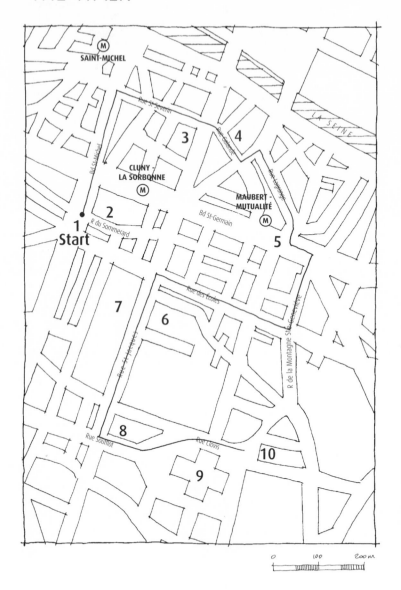

SAINT-MICHEL

Rue St-Severin

LA SEINE

3

4

Bd St-Michel

CLUNY -
LA SORBONNE

Rue Galande

Rue Lagrange

MAUBERT -
MUTUALITÉ

Bd St-Germain

2

1
Start

R du Sommerard

5

Rue des Écoles

7

6

Rue St-Jacques

R de la Montagne Ste-Geneviève

8

Rue Soufflot

Rue Clovis

10

9

0   100   200 m

KEY

1. Boulevard St-Michel
2. Musée Nationale du Moyen Age
3. St-Séverin
4. St-Julien-le-Pauvre
5. Place Maubert
6. Collège de France
7. La Sorbonne
8. Bibliothèque Sainte-Geneviève
9. Panthéon
10. St-Etienne-du-Mont

Latin Quarter

Boulevard St-Michel ❶

Leave the Cluny La Sorbonne metro station and walk to Boulevard St-Michel, the main thoroughfare through the Latin Quarter. It was created by Baron Haussmann in 1869, and runs 1.4 kilometres southwards from the Pont St-Michel, from which it gets its name. Cutting through the medieval fabric of this part of the city, the boulevard runs all the way to Place Camille Jullian, and parallel to the old Roman road now known as rue St-Jacques. This traditionally formed the north-south axis of the city. Famed for its literary cafés, these have largely been replaced by cheap shops and fast-food restaurants.

Affectionately known as Boul'Mich, it has a long history of student activism, particularly the students riots that erupted in 1968. Place St-Michel contains the **Fontaine St-Michel**. Constructed by Gabriel Davioud between 1855 and 1860, the fountain's original statue was supposed to depict Napoleon, but public opposition caused it to be replaced by the less controversial figure of the archangel St Michel. The saint is depicted with two dragons – spouting water rather than breathing fire – and four figures representing the classical virtues of justice, prudence, temperance and fortitude. Place St-Michel also contains a marble plaque commemorating the students who died fighting the German occupation here in 1944.

Musée Nationale du Moyen Age ❷

Turn off Boulevard St-Michel onto rue du Sommerard and the Musée Nationale du Moyen Age will be on your left at No. 6 Place Paul-Painlevé. This was known as the Musée de Cluny until recently, in honour of the building's original owner, Pierre de Châlus, who was Abbot of Cluny. He bought the site in 1330, when it contained nothing more than some ruins (these were later discovered to be from the Gallo-Roman era). The building was built and extended many times until it was finally completed in 1550 by another abbot, Jacques d'Amboise.

Alexandre du Sommerard took it over in 1833 to house his impressive art collection, which he then willed to the state. This is one of the world's finest collections of medieval art and is housed across the two floors of the building. Covering a wide range of items, it includes manuscripts, tapestries and other textiles, as well as precious metals, ceramics and sculpture. Some of the collection's highlights include a magnificent 15th-century *Book of Hours* and the famous *Lady with the Unicorn* tapestries, woven in the southern Netherlands in the late 15th century and remarkable for their sensitive depiction of plants, animals and people. There are also some wonderful religious carvings and stained glass, some of which come from the Basilique St-Denis and date back to the 12th century. Of particular interest are the everyday objects from the Middle Ages, including kitchenware, clothing and children's toys. One of the museum's most precious exhibits is the *Golden Rose of Basle*, a delicate monstrance which dates to 1330, making it the oldest of its kind in the world. It was made by the goldsmith Minucchio da Siena for use by Pope John XXII in Avignon.

Cluny is also the site of the **Gallo-Roman baths**, which rank as the oldest interior in the city. Dating from c.215 CE, the reign of Caracalla, these were sacked by barbarian invaders and eventually demolished during the Norman era. The ruins then disappeared for centuries before being rediscovered in 1819, but it was only in 1837 that they were recognised for what they were. Opened to the public in 1844, the baths' vaulted *frigidarium* (cold bath) was the largest of its kind in France and contains arches that date back to the 1st and 2nd centuries CE. These were decorated with pairs of carved ship prows, a symbol of the Seine boatmen (the *nautes*). There are also ruins of the *caldarium* and *tepidarium* (hot and tepid baths).

Musée Nationale du Moyen Age
Opening times: 9.15am–5.45pm Wed–Mon
Closed 1 Jan, 1 May, 25 Dec
Website: www.musee-moyenage.fr
Tel: 01. 53 73 78 16

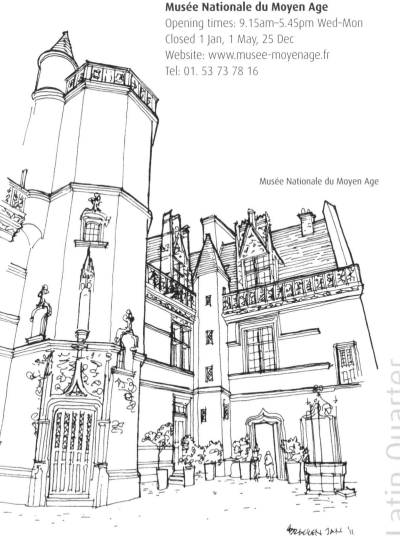

Musée Nationale du Moyen Age

Latin Quarter

St-Séverin ❸

Retrace your steps to the Boulevard St-Michel and turn right, follow it until you come to rue St-Séverin and turn right again and the church of St-Séverin will be straight in front of you. Built at the beginning of the 13th century on the site of an earlier chapel which dated from 650, this is one of the most beautiful churches in Paris and an excellent example of the Gothic style. It was finally completed in 1530 and contains some excellent stained glass dating from the end of the 14th and early 15th centuries. The interior also includes a remarkable double ambulatory which circles the chancel. Named after a 6th-century hermit who lived in the area, he is reputed to have been responsible for encouraging St Cloud, the grandson of King Clovis, to take holy orders. The chancel was modernised after the Grande Mademoiselle, a cousin of Louis XIV, adopted the church as her parish church after breaking with St-Sulpice in 1684.

A small garden accessible from the church's interior stands on what used to be burial grounds and there is also a medieval gable-roofed charnel house here. The church frequently hosts concerts. Nearby at **No. 22 rue St-Séverin** you will find what is reputed to be the narrowest house in Paris. It used to be the residence of Abbé Prévost, the author of *Manon Lescaut*.

St-Séverin

Opening times: 11am–7.30pm daily
Tel: 01. 42 34 93 50

Did You Know?

The garden of St-Séverin was the site of the first operation ever for gall stones. This took place in 1474 after King Louis XI offered an archer who had been condemned to death the chance of freedom if he consented to it. He did, and it was a success – the archer went free, and was cured in the bargain.

St-Julien-le-Pauvre ❹

Leave St-Séverin and turn right and right again, then keeping the side of the church on your right, follow it and you will see St-Julien-le-Pauvre in front of you after the junction with rue St-Jacques. Built between 1165 and 1240, this is one of the oldest churches in the city.

Located at a strategic point, adjacent to the central islands and between the two main routes south to Orleans and Lyons, it is a surprisingly modest structure. There are at least three saints who can claim to be its patron, but St Julian Hospitaller is the most likely. It was used for university meetings until 1524, when a student protest created so much damage that they were banned from using the church by an act of parliament. It was used as

a store for animal feed during the Revolution and then lay idle for nearly a century before being established as a Greek Orthodox place of worship in 1889. It is frequently used for concerts of religious and chamber music.

The church's tower dates back to the 12th century but was never finished. The interior has some quite interesting capitals in the choir, while the wooden marquetry was completed in 1901 by an artisan called Damas. The **Shakespeare & Co** bookstore is located nearby at No. 37 rue de la Bûcherie, having moved here from its original location on rue de l'Odéon.

St-Julien-le-Pauvre
Opening times: 9.30am–1.30pm, 3–6pm daily
Tel: 01. 43 54 52 16

Place Maubert ❺

Leaving St-Julien-le-Pauvre turn left and left again onto **rue Galande**. This street was originally a very chic location but became notorious for its taverns after the 17th century. Turn left on rue Dante and right onto rue Monge and you will come to Place Maubert. 'La Maub', as it was known, was one of the city's most important scholastic centres in the Middle Ages.

From the 12th to the middle of the 13th century, it used to host open-air lectures where the students would sit on straw in the street. **Rue du Fouarre** takes its name from these lectures – *fouarre* meaning straw in French. After the scholars moved to the new university buildings that were being built nearby, **Place Maubert** became a place of torture and execution. Philosopher Etienne Dolet was burned at the stake here in 1546, as were many Protestants, so much so that it became a place of pilgrimage. This dark chapter in the Place Maubert's history has been replaced by a new zest for life, and the square is now home to a lively street market.

Cross Place Maubert and turn up rue de la Montagne Ste-Geneviève, the **Musée de la Préfecture de Police** will be at No. 4. This shows a return to the darker side of Paris life. This rather small, old-fashioned museum traces the development of the Paris police force from medieval times right up to the 20th century. Created in 1909, its exhibits include arrest warrants for famous figures, such as the revolutionary Danton, as well as weapons and tools used by infamous criminals. There is also a section highlighting the role the police played in the Resistance and Liberation of Paris.

Musée de la Préfecture de Police
Opening times: 9am–5pm Mon–Fri; 10am–5pm Sat (last admission 4.30pm)
Closed public hols
Tel: 01. 44 41 52 50

Latin Quarter

Collège de France

Collège de France ❻

Continue up rue de la Montagne Ste-Geneviève and turn right onto rue des Écoles and the Collège de France will on your left, up the steps at No. 11 Place Marcelin-Berthelot. This is one of Paris' great institutes of learning, established in 1530 by François I, under the encouragement of the humanist Guillaume Budé. The king was trying to counteract the intolerance and dogmatism of the neighbouring Sorbonne. There is a statue of Budé in the western courtyard, a man whose unbiased approach to learning is reflected in the inscription over the college entrance: *docet omnia* (all are taught here). Lectures are still free and open to anyone who cares to attend.

Collège de France
Opening times: 9am–6pm Mon–Fri, Oct–Jun
Tel: 01. 44 27 12 11

La Sorbonne

La Sorbonne is across rue St-Jacques from the Collège de France at No. 47 rue des Écoles. Established in 1257, this is the seat of the venerable University of Paris. Founded by Robert de Sorbon, who was confessor to Louis IX, it was intended to educate the poor in theology. It began with 16 lucky souls and grew to become a major international centre of theological study. The University's rector established three printing machines in 1469, having brought them over from Mainz, thus establishing France's first printing press. The college was suppressed during the Revolution thanks to its long-standing opposition to the traditions of 18th-century liberalism. It was re-established as a place of learning by Napoleon in 1806.

The college buildings were originally built by Cardinal Richelieu in the early 17th century, but these have all been replaced by the Renaissance style blocks we see today. The only exception to this is the **Chapelle de la Sorbonne**. This monument to Richelieu was designed by Lemercier and built between 1635 and 1642. The Cardinal's coat-of-arms can be seen on the dome's supports while his white marble tomb, carved by Girardon in 1694, lies in the chancel. The Chapelle looks out onto the Sorbonne's main courtyard.

La Sorbonne
Opening times: 9am–5pm Mon–Fri
Closed public hols
Tel: 01. 40 46 22 11

Chapelle de la Sorbonne
Open for temporary exhibitions only

La Sorbonne

Bibliothèque Sainte-Geneviève ❽

Walk up rue St-Jacques and turn left onto rue Sufflot. The Bibliothèque Sainte-Geneviève will be on your left at No. 10 Place du Panthéon. A groundbreaking structure, and one of the great cultural buildings of the 19th century, it was the first building to use iron in a prominent, visible way. Designed by Henri Labrouste in 1838–39, the Bibliothèque was built between 1843 and 1850. It inherited the collection of one of the largest and oldest abbeys in Paris, Sainte-Geneviève. This had been a Benedictine Abbey founded by Clovis I in the 6th century and initially devoted to the Apostles Peter and Paul. It changed its name in 512 when it received the body of the patron saint of Paris.

The Bibliothèque Sainte-Geneviève consists of a large two-storey structure that fills a wide, shallow site in a deceptively simple way. The lower floor is filled with book stacks, storage and office space, and centres on a vestibule that leads via a spacious staircase to the upper-story reading room. This reading room is somewhat reminiscent of the refectory in the 13th-century St-Martin Priory and takes up the entire upper storey. It is split by a spine of slender, cast-iron columns in the Ionic order that divides the space in two. These columns support openwork iron arches that carry the barrel vaulted ceiling of plaster reinforced by iron mesh. The windows are oriented east and west to capture the morning and evening light, and this is reflected in the decoration on the columns' plinths, which represent Day and Night on alternate sides. Long regarded as one of the masterpieces of 19th-century architecture, its simple utilitarianism has been hugely influential. The only real decoration in the whole building is the series of names carved into the façade in 1848. These consists of 810 authors' names, ranging from Moses to a Swedish chemist called Berzelius who died that year.

Bibliothèque Sainte-Geneviève
Opening times: 10am–10pm Mon–Sat
Website: www.bsg.univ-paris1.fr
Tel: 01. 44 41 97 97

Panthéon ❾

At the proud centre of Place du Panthéon stands this famous building. Louis XV suffered from a serious illness in 1744 and was so glad to have recovered that he decided to build a magnificent church dedicated to Sainte Geneviève.

Jacques-Germain Soufflot was the fourteenth child of a provincial lawyer who had refused to follow his father into the profession and went instead to Rome to study architecture. His design for a Hôtel-Dieu (hospice) in Lyons caught the eye of Madame de Pompadour in 1740, and it was she who was instrumental in getting Sufflot this great commission.

Intended to rival St Peter's in Rome and St Paul's in London, this magnificent example of Enlightenment architecture was revolutionary in that it was built on the plan of a Greek cross, not the more usual Christian one with its

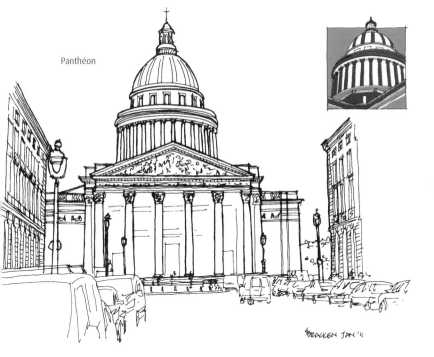

Panthéon

elongated nave (a design that both Michelangelo and Sir Christopher Wren failed to convince their clients to approve of when they were building their own magnificent cathedrals as it went against the tenets of traditional church design). Soufflot's Neoclassical masterpiece replaced an old abbey church, which was in bad condition, and sits atop Mont Ste-Geneviève, the high point of the Left Bank. Construction began in 1764 and was completed by 1790, ten years after Sufflot's death, under the supervision of Guillaume Rondelet. The Revolution was already underway so the church found itself turned into a pantheon – a location for the tombs of the country's great and good.

Napoleon returned the church to religious use in 1806, but it was resecularised and then desecularised once again before finally being turned into a civic building in 1885. The people buried here also reflect something of this national schizophrenia. The popular orator Honoré Mirabeau was the first to be installed, only to be removed by Robespierre. Voltaire is also buried here, and there is a statue of the great man by Jean-Antoine Houdon in front of his tomb. Other honourees include Jean-Jacques Rousseau, Victor Hugo and Emile Zola. Pierre and Marie Curie's remains were transferred here in 1995, with Malraux's following in 1996. The façade is inspired by Rome's Pantheon, with a temple portico of 22 Corinthian columns.

The pediment relief is by David d'Angers and depicts France granting laurels to her great men. The colonnade encircling the dome is both a decorative feature and part of an ingenious structural support system. The dome, with its stone cupola, is 83 metres (272 feet) high and was inspired by St Paul's in London as well as the Dôme church. Its galleries command wonderful views of the city. The lantern allows only a little light to filter through as too bright a space was thought inappropriate for the resting place of France's finest. The

Latin Quarter

dome's arches were designed by Rondelet and show a renewed interest in the lightness of Gothic architecture. The frescoes of Sainte Geneviève along the south wall of the nave date from the 19th century and are by Puvis de Chavannes. Sufflot's innovation was to construct his building using rational scientific formulae, which eliminated the need for supporting piers and resulting in the interior's slender and elegant vaulting. However, his faith in the new scientific methods was somewhat misplaced as cracks soon began to appear and the structural piers had to be thickened. A number of the windows were also blocked to add to the building's structural integrity.

Panthéon
Opening times: 10am–6.30pm daily, Apr–Sept; 10am–6pm daily, Oct–Mar
Closed 1 Jan, 1 May, 25 Dec
Tel: 01. 44 32 18 00

Did You Know?
The Panthéon was the location for Foucault's famous pendulum experiment in 1851 that demonstrated the rotation of the earth.

St-Etienne-du-Mont ⑩

Located on Place Ste-Geneviève just behind the Panthéon to the north is the church of St-Etienne-du-Mont. This beautiful church began life as part of the Abbey of Ste-Geneviève and still contains a shrine to the patron saint of Paris. The name St Etienne comes from the patron saint of the old 13th-century Cathedral of Paris.

St-Etienne-du-Mont was enlarged and extended many times until a new church was begun in 1492 by architect Stephen Viguier. This was in a flamboyant Gothic style and was completed in 1537. It was further altered during the Renaissance, when the nave was reconstructed (in 1584) and the current church façade was begun in 1610, thanks to a substantial donation by Marguerite de Valois.

A prestigious church until the Revolution, it was first closed, and then opened as a temple of filial piety. Normal worship resumed in 1801 and the remains of some great literary figures can be found here, such as Racine and Pascal. Marat is also buried in the church's cemetery.

St-Etienne-du-Mont
Opening times: 8.45am–7.30pm Tue–Fri, noon–7.30pm Mon,
weekend closed midday.
Closed Mon in Jul and Aug
Tel: 01. 43 54 11 79

Link to the Jardin des Plantes walk: Walk along rue Clovis until you come to rue du Cardinal Lemoine and turn left. Then take a right onto rue Monge.

Jardin des Plantes

Nearest Metro: Cardinal Lemoine
Approximate walking time: 2 hours

Jardin des Plantes

This is an area seldom visited by tourists, yet it is full of treasures, from an ancient Gallo-Roman arena to one of the best shopping streets in the city: rue Mouffetard. This delightful old street has a number of open-air markets well known for their fresh produce. The area is also home to Paris' botanical gardens, the Jardin des Plantes, which were established by two doctors for medicinal herbs during the reign of Louis XIII. Parts of the area seem to have remained unchanged for centuries, giving it a curiously timeless feel, but it also has some cutting-edge architecture in the form of the Institute du Monde Arabe, which overlooks the Seine near the historic islands.

THE WALK

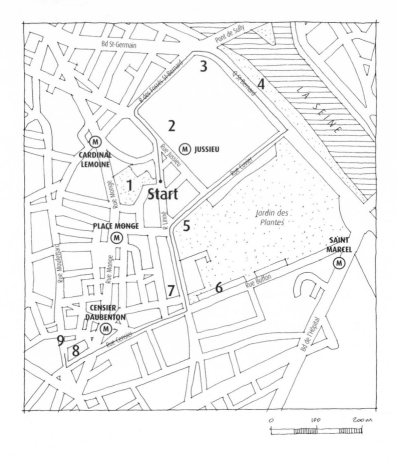

Bd St-Germain

Pont de Sully

3

R des Fossés St-Bernard

Q St-Bernard

4

LA SEINE

2

(M) JUSSIEU

Rue Jussieu

(M)
CARDINAL
LEMOINE

Rue Monge

1

Start

Rue Cuvier

Jardin des
Plantes

R Linné

5

PLACE MONGE
(M)

SAINT
MARCEL
(M)

Rue Mouffetard

Rue Monge

7

6

Rue Buffon

Bd de l'Hôpital

CENSIER
DAUBENTON
(M)

9

Rue Censier

8

0   100   200 m

KEY

1. Arènes de Lutèce
2. Collection des Minéraux de l'Université
3. Institute du Monde Arabe
4. Musée de la Sculpture en Plein Air
5. Jardin des Plantes
6. Musée Nationale d'Histoire Naturelle
7. Mosquée de Paris
8. St-Médard
9. Rue Mouffetard

Jardin des Plantes

Arènes de Lutèce

Arènes de Lutèce ❶

Leave the Cardinal Lemoine metro station and follow rue Monge south and you will come to the Arènes de Lutèce on your left. With a capacity of 15,000, this Gallo-Roman amphitheatre dates from the end of the 2nd century and would have been used for theatrical performances as well as gladiatorial combat. Lutetia was the Roman name for Paris. After Paris was attacked by barbarians in the 3rd century the Romans left and parts of the old arena were carted off for use in the new city walls being constructed on the Ile de la Cité. The rest of the arena was slowly buried over the centuries before being rediscovered in 1869 when rue Monge was being built. A restoration campaign began, championed by people such as Victor Hugo, but restoration work did not really get underway until after World War I.

The arena had 35 tiers of seats and was typical of the Roman amphitheatres built in Gaul (the Roman name for France), it is very similar to the ones at Nîmes and Arles. Attached to the old arena is a pretty little park which contains a spectacular double stone staircase which sweeps symmetrically down to a lower level. Overlooking the park is **No. 5 rue des Arènes**, an interesting-looking Gothic house which was the home of writer Jean Paulhan from 1940 until his death 28 years later.

Collection des Minéraux de l'Université ❷

Exit the Arènes de Lutèce via rue Linné and turn left. When you come to rue Jussieu the **Jussieu Campus** of the Pierre and Marie Curie University will be ahead of you. The imposing **Zamansky Tower** rises to a height of 85 metres (280 feet), dominating the entrance. The campus opened in 1959 on the location of a wine market set up by Napoleon. It is home to most of the Sorbonne's faculty of sciences. Soon after it opened it became apparent that a much bigger campus was needed, so architect Edouard Albert designed this rigid grid of 6-storey blocks in 1964. They sit on stilts over a massive slab containing an underground car park and some of the campus' ancillary facilities.

The **Collection des Minéraux de l'Université** (University's Mineral Collection) is a small but fascinating museum housed in the main building at No. 4 Place Jussieu. The collection comprises precious stones, both cut and uncut, as well as rock crystal from around the world. These are displayed to maximum effect by the use of clever lighting.

Collection des Minéraux de l'Université
Opening times: 1–6pm Wed–Mon
Closed 1 Jan, Easter, 1 May, 14 Jul, 1 Nov, 25 Dec
Tel: 01. 44 27 52 88

Zamansky Tower

Jardin des Plantes

> **Did You Know?**
> In order to allow the old Napoleonic wine market to remain in place, the architect of the new Jussieu Campus planned the buildings on stilts so they wouldn't interfere with its workings.

Institute du Monde Arabe ❸

Walk along rue des Fossées St-Bernard and the Institute du Monde Arabe will be on your right at the end of the road. This masterpiece of French High-tech architecture is by Jean Nouvel (who is also responsible for the Musée de Quai Branly). It combines modern materials in the spirit of traditional Arab culture and won the prestigious Aga Khan Award. Founded in 1980 as a cultural institution by the French in partnership with 20 Arab countries, it was established to foster cultural ties between the West and the Islamic world. It was also an effort on France's part to make up for the problematic relationship with former North African colonies.

The building's south elevation is its most famous feature, consisting of 1,600 high-tech metal screens which act as light filters, they control how much light enters the building. Based on the *moucharabiyahs* (carved wooden screens) that are found throughout the Arab world, each screen contains 21 electronically-controlled irises which open and close depending on how much light hits their photosensitive cells. The central iris is made up of interlocking metal blades which open and close like the shutter of a camera. When they work, the irises create delicate patterns of light and shade in the building's interior.

The interior also contains an enclosed courtyard reached by the narrow gap that splits the building in two. From floors four to seven a fascinating display of Islamic artwork is to be seen. Dating from the 9th to the 19th centuries, this includes glassware, ceramics, sculpture, carpets and even astrolabes (a type of astronomical instrument). The white marble book-tower is reminiscent of a mosque's minaret, while the rest of the building contains a library and media archive. The north façade, facing the Seine, has a stylised silk-screen reproduction of the skyline it faces, which acts as a sort of mirror to this part of the city. The south side opens onto the plaza connecting the institute to the Jussieu Campus.

Institute du Monde Arabe
Opening times: Museum and temporary exhibitions: 10am–6pm Tue–Sun
Library: 1–8pm Tue–Sat
Website: www.imarabe.org
Tel: 01. 40 51 38 38

Musée de la Sculpture en Plein Air ❹

Continue along rue des Fossées St-Bernard and you will come to the River Seine. The Pont de Sully crosses the river at this point, linking both sides of it via the Ile St-Louis. Opened in 1877, this cast-iron bridge is not particularly remarkable, but it is a wonderful place to enjoy views of the islands and Notre-Dame in the distance beyond the lovely Pont de la Tournelle.

Walk along Quai St-Bernard and the **Musée de la Sculpture en Plein Air** will be on your left. Opened in 1975, this open-air sculpture park overlooking the river contains some interesting pieces. Some of the more valuable ones had to be removed to protect them from vandalism. The sculpture garden is named after Tino Rossi, a Corsican singer famous in France, and runs along Quai St-Bernard. It's a pleasant place for a quiet stroll along the river's edge.

Did You Know?
In the 17th century Quai St-Bernard was infamous for its nude bathing. Eventually the city authorities were obliged to ban the practice to silence the protests from the scandalised public of Paris.

Jardin des Plantes ❺

Turn right onto rue Cuvier. This long, straight road feels like a country lane. The **Cuvier Fountain** will be at the end on your right. A memorial to the famous naturalist Georges Cuvier, the father of palaeontology, the fountain was installed in 1840. Designed by Vigouroux it contains carvings by Jean-Jacques Feuchère. The entrance to the **Jardin des Plantes** (botanical gardens) is opposite the fountain. One of Paris' great parks, the gardens were established in 1626 by two of Louis XIII's physicians, Jean Hérouard and Guy de la Brosse. They were given permission to start a medicinal herb garden here. They chose this part of the city because it was quiet, and also because of its proximity to a number of other herb gardens that belonged to different religious orders.

The gardens were opened to the public in 1640 and now include schools of botany, natural history and pharmacy. It also includes a natural history museum, a botanical school and a zoo. Lovely walkways wind their way through ancient woods and afford excellent views over the lawns and the garden's many statues. The park also contains the first cedar of Lebanon planted in France, which came from Kew Gardens in London. There is also a fascinating Alpine garden with plants from diverse mountainous places such as Corsica, Morocco, the Alps and the Himalayas.

The entrance to Jardin des Plantes' **Ménagerie** or zoo is at No. 57 rue Cuvier. This is France's oldest zoological gardens and was established during the Revolution to house the animals rescued from the royal menagerie at Versailles – all four of them. The state then set about rounding up circus animals and other exotic creatures that had been sent to the country from abroad. The Ménagerie is a great favourite with children as it is possible to get quite close to the animals. The zoo contains a large primate house, a vivarium (where live animals can be seen in their natural habitats) and an excellent collection of insects. There is also a large waterfowl aviary and a big cat house that is home to some Chinese panthers.

Jardin des Plantes
Opening times: 8am–6.45pm (till 5.45pm in winter) daily

Ménagerie
Opening times: 9am–5.30pm daily

Did You Know?
All the animals in the Jardin des Plantes' zoo were eaten during the siege of Paris in 1870.

Muséum Nationale d'Histoire Naturelle ❻

The Muséum Nationale d'Histoire Naturelle (National Museum of Natural History) forms part of the Jardin des Plantes complex and can also be entered from No. 2 rue Buffon. The highlight of this excellent museum is the Grande Galerie d'Evolution (Great Gallery of Evolution). The four other departments are zoology, botany, geology and palaeontology. Housed in an impressive Beaux Arts building, they show skeletons and plaster-casts of various animals, fossils of plants, gemstones and fossilised insects. The bookshop is housed in the former home of the Jardin des Plantes' most famous director, the naturalist Buffon, who lived here from 1772 until his death in 1788. There is a memorial statue to him in the garden in front of the museum.

Muséum Nationale d'Histoire Naturelle
Opening times: 10am–6pm Wed–Mon
Closed 1 May
Tel: 01. 40 79 56 01

Mosquée de Paris ❼

Across rue Geoffrey St-Hilaire from the Jardin des Plantes sits the Mosquée de Paris. Built on land donated by the City of Paris and partially financed by the French state, this beautiful mosque was built between 1922 and 1926. Architects Robert Fournez, Maurice Mantout and Charles Heubes based their designs on plans that had been drawn up by Maurice Tranchant de Lunel, who was chief of the Beaux Arts service in Morocco. It acts as a memorial to the 100,000 Muslim soldiers who died fighting for France during World War I.

At the heart of the building is a great courtyard surrounded by colonnades containing mosaics and arches with delicate fretwork. The courtyard makes use of scented eucalyptus and cedar wood and is modelled on the Alhambra in Granada. Once used by scholars, the mosque has grown to become the spiritual heart of the city's Muslim population. It is also home to the Grand Imam. Each of the mosque's domes is decorated in a different style, and the white-walled, green-roofed complex is crowned by a minaret rising 33 metres (108 feet) into the air. Made of reinforced concrete, the mosque is beautifully decorated with mosaics, faience and wrought iron. The plaster moulding and wood carvings feature Islamic calligraphy.

The mosque forms part of a larger complex that houses religious, educational and commercial facilities and even has a Hammam, or Turkish bath, which can be enjoyed by men and women on alternate days. There is also a lovely tearoom serving Moorish specialities.

Mosquée de Paris
Opening times: 9am–noon, 2–6pm Sat–Thur
Closed Muslim hols
Website: www.mosquee-de-paris.com
Tel: 01. 45 35 97 33

Tearoom and Turkish baths
Tel: 01. 43 31 38 20

Mosquée de Paris

Jardin des Plantes

St-Médard

Turn right onto rue Censier and you will come to the church of St-Médard on your right, at the bottom of rue Mouffetard. St Médard was a counsellor to the Merovingian kings and was famous for his custom of giving wreaths of white roses to girls of conspicuous virtue. This present church was begun in the mid-15th century on the foundations of an older Romanesque place of worship. Construction was halted a number of times, including when the building was stormed by angry Protestants in 1561, during the Wars of Religion.

In 1655 it became the parish church of the Faubourg St-Marcel and in 1784 a choir was installed in Neoclassical style. The nave's 16th-century stained-glass windows were replaced at the same time. During the Revolution the church was designated a Temple of Work. The interior has a number of good paintings, including Francisco de Zurbaran's *St Joseph Walking with the Christ Child*. The churchyard, which is now a pretty garden, was notorious in the 18th century as a place where the Convulsionnaires, an hysterical Catholic sect, would indulge in fits brought on by the contemplation of miracles.

St-Médard

Opening times: 8am–noon, 2.30–7pm Tue–Sat,
4–7pm Sun
Tel: 01. 44 08 87 00

Rue Mouffetard

'La Mouffe', as it is known to the locals, is famous for its open-air markets, particularly those on Place Maubert, Place Monge and the rue Daubenton (which is a side street and home to a lively African market). This roadway has been in use since Roman times, which makes it one of the oldest in the city, and still retains a somewhat medieval air. It is possible to catch a glimpse of what life must have been like back then, with markets, shops and churches all huddled together along a winding, sloping street. Some of the smaller shops even still sport ancient-looking painted signs advertising their wares. In the 17th and 18th centuries the street was known as the Grande Rue du Faubourg St-Marcel and a number of the buildings date from this time. No. 125 has a restored Louis XIII façade, while the front of No. 134 is worth watching for because of its remarkable decoration featuring wild animals, plants and flowers.

The **Passage des Postes** is an ancient alleyway that was opened onto rue Mouffetard in 1830, while the **Pot de Fer** is one of 14 fountains Marie de Medicis had built on the Left Bank in 1624 to provide water for her Palais du Luxembourg. The fountain was rebuilt in 1671. **Place de la Contrescarpe** was laid out in 1852 and used to lie outside the old city walls. It got its name from the moat that ran along these walls, built by King Philipp-Auguste at the beginning of the 13th century.

This area has long been home to festivals and is still extremely lively, especially on weekends. There is a famous Bastille Day Ball held here each year. No. 1 Place de la Contrescarpe has a plaque commemorating the 'Pine-cone Club' immortalised by Rabelais, and was where a group of writers called *La Pléiade* (The Pleiades – after the constellation) used to meet in the 16th century.

Rue Mouffetard

Jardin des Plantes

Rue Mouffetard Markets

Place Maubert

Opening times: 7am–2.30pm Tue and Thur, 7am–3pm Sat

Place Monge

Opening times: 7am–2.30 Wed and Fri, 7am–3pm Sun

Did You Know?

A hoard of gold coins was found at No. 53 rue Mouffetard when the house was being demolished in 1938. Dating from the 18th century, these *louis* would have been hidden away by a careful hoarder who either died too early to tell anyone about them, or was too mean to.

Link to the Luxembourg walk: From the St-Médard end of rue Mouffetard walk up rue Claude Bernard, which turns into rue des Feuillantines. Then turn left onto rue St-Jacques.

Luxembourg

Nearest Metro: Vavin
Approximate walking time: 2 hours

Luxembourg

The area around the Jardin du Luxembourg is one of the most sought-after in the city. It is close to the bustle of St-Germain-des-Prés, but its quiet leafy greenness make it seem a world away. The gardens of the Palais du Luxembourg were opened to the public in the 19th century, when people used to be able to pick the fruit in the orchards on payment of a small fee. The gardens are a beautifully planted series of formal walkways, avenues and ponds popular with tourists and locals alike. The area around the gardens is full of interesting buildings, including the churches of St-Sulpice, St-Joseph-des-Carmes and Val-de-Grâce, this last one reckoned to be the most beautiful in the city. There are also two famous fountains: the de Medicis and de l'Observatoire, both of which are spectacular sites for a city centre. Then there is the Observatoire de Paris as well as the Ecole Nationale Supérieure des Mines, one of France's most prestigious research and education establishments.

THE WALK

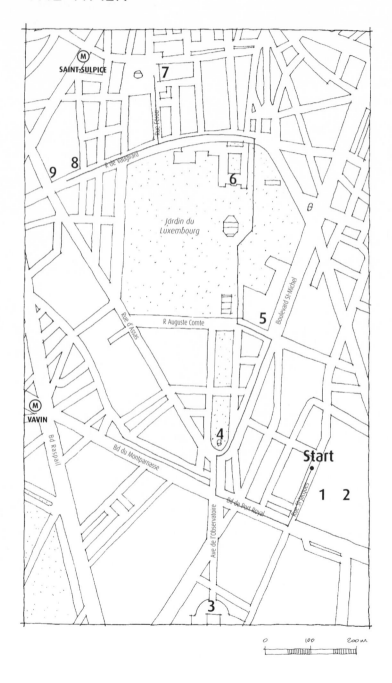

SAINT-SULPICE (M)

7

Rue Férou

R de Vaugirard

8

9

6

Jardin du
Luxembourg

θ

Boulevard St-Michel

Rue d'Assas

R Auguste Comte

5

VAVIN (M)

Bd Raspail

Bd du Montparnasse

4

Start

●

1   2

Rue St-Jacques

Ave de l'Observatoire

Bd de Port Royal

3

0   100   200 m

KEY

1. Val-de-Grâce
2. Musée du Service de Santé des Armées
3. Observatoire de Paris
4. Fontaine de l'Observatoire
5. Ecole Nationale Supérieure des Mines
6. Palais du Luxembourg
7. St-Sulpice
8. St-Joseph-des-Carmes
9. Institute Catholique de Paris

Luxembourg

Val-de-Grâce ❶

Leave the Vavin metro station and follow Boulevard de Montparnasse, which turns into Boulevard de Port Royal and then turn left onto rue St-Jacques. This will be a rather long walk, as there are no metro stations particularly close to the start of this walk. Val-de-Grâce will be on your right. This is regarded as one of the most beautiful churches in Paris. It was built for Anne of Austria (wife of Louis XIII) in thanks to the Blessed Virgin for having given birth to a son after 23 years of childless marriage. The son went on to become King Louis XIV, the Sun King. The seven-year-old Louis is said to have laid the church's foundation stone in 1645.

Designed by François Mansart and Jacques Lemercier, Val-de-Grâce is a magnificent example of Baroque architecture. Completed in 1667, the church's beautiful lead-and-gilt dome is 41 metres (135 feet) high and 19 metres (62 feet) in diameter. The interior of the dome is painted with over 200 triple-life-size figures by Pierre Mignard. The six twisting marble columns that frame the high altar are modelled on Bernini's in St Peter's in Rome. 26 members of the French royal family are buried here, including both the Bourbon and the Orléans branches. Unlike many churches in the city, this one survived the Revolution intact, mainly because of the Benedictine nuns who were providing medical care to injured revolutionaries. This tradition of care is continued here today, as the church is part of a military hospital complex.

Val-de-Grâce
Opening times: Noon–6pm Tue, Wed, Sat and Sun
Website: www.valdegrace.org
Tel: 01. 40 51 51 9251 92

Val-de-Grâce

Musée du Service de Santé des Armées ❷

Next door to Val-de-Grâce, and in the same compound, is the Musée du Service de Santé des Armées. These buildings, in the west wing of the Val-de-Grâce church, were converted from an abbey into a military hospital after the Revolution in 1795. The Musée du Val-de-Grâce was established during World War I and is run by the army medical corps. Its exhibits show the history of medicine, with artificial limbs and surgical instruments. The complex's original buildings now serve as offices and teaching facilities, while the actual medical facilities are located in another building, to the east, which is larger and dates from the 1970s. This is where France's top officials go for medical treatment. Note, as this is a military facility, cameras are not allowed.

Musée du Service de Santé des Armées
Opening times: Noon–6pm Tue, Wed, Sat and Sun
Tel: 01. 40 51 51 92

Luxembourg

Observatoire de Paris ❸

Retrace your steps to Boulevard de Port Royal and turn right, then take a left onto Avenue de l'Observatoire and the Observatoire de Paris will be straight ahead of you. Louis XIV was persuaded by scientists and astronomers that the country needed a royal observatory, so he founded one here in 1666. It has two other branches (in Meudon and Nançay) and employs about 800 staff. It is also one of the world's most renowned astronomical research institutes. Building began on 21 June 1666, the summer solstice, and was completed within five years. Designed by Claude Perrault, and built for purely practical scientific research, the observatory still manages to achieve an elegance and lightness of touch that belies this simple functionality. Sitting on the grand axis that runs to the Palais du Luxembourg, some of the astronomical research undertaken here includes the calculation of the exact dimension of the solar system (in 1672), the mapping of the moon (1679), and the discovery of the planet Neptune (1846).

Observatoire de Paris
Opening times: 1st Sat of month, 2.30pm for two hours, apply two months ahead, groups by appointment
Closed August
Website: www.obspm.fr
Tel: 01. 45 07 74 78 (2–4pm Mon–Fri)

Fontaine de l'Observatoire ❹

With your back to the Observatoire de Paris walk up Avenue de l'Observatoire and you will come to the Fontaine de l'Observatoire. This monumental fountain sits on the axis that runs north from the observatory through the Jardin du Luxembourg up to the Palais du Luxembourg. Also known as the Fontaine des Quatre-Parties-du-Monde (Fountain of the Four Parts of the World) this bronze sculpture features four women supporting an open globe. These represent the four continents of Europe, Asia, Africa and America (the fifth, Oceania, was left out so that the fountain could be more symmetrical). Designed by Jean-Baptiste Carpeaux, it was finally finished in 1874, having been delayed due to the Franco-Prussian War of 1870–71. The horses were sculpted by Emmanuel Frémiet.

The idea of a fountain was first proposed by Baron Haussmann in 1866. It was intended to be part of his grand new avenue for this part of the city. The fountain had to be something imposing enough to make itself felt, but not so huge that it would obscure the views of either the dome of the observatory or the Palais du Luxembourg. Carpeaux died the year after the fountain was finished; he had been in poor health, but the adverse critical reception to it may not have helped.

Ecole Nationale Supérieure des Mines

Walk up Boulevard St-Michel and the Ecole Nationale Supérieure des Mines will be on your left at No. 60. Founded by Louis XVI in 1783, the School of Mines was established to train mining engineers. It is now one of the country's Grands Ecoles and despite its small size – it only accepts 120 students a year – it is one of the country's most prestigious educational establishments. Initially located in the Hôtel de la Monnaie overlooking the River Seine, it closed down during the Revolution. It was re-established in 1794 but moved to Savoie. After the Bourbon restoration in 1814 it moved back to the city and was established here in the Hôtel de Vendôme. The school is also home to the Musée de Minéralogie, a national collection of minerals.

Ecole Nationale Supérieure des Mines
Opening times: 1.30–6pm Tue–Fri; 10am–12.30pm, 2–5pm Sat
Tel: 01. 40 51 91 39

Palais du Luxembourg

Enter the **Jardin du Luxembourg** via rue Auguste Comte. These magnificent gardens cover 25 hectares (60 acres) and stand on what used to be a Carthusian monastery. The gardens are centred on the Palais du Luxembourg and a vast octagonal pool, the Grand Bassin. Attributed to François Chalgrin, this is popular with children sailing toy boats.

Most of the garden's 60 statues were erected in the 19th century. These include queens of France (circling the main fountain), George Sand by Sicard and Stendhal by Rodin (both of which are near the main entrance on Boulevard St-Michel). There is also a bust of Beethoven by Bourdelle, near the corner of rue de Vaugirard and rue Guynemer.

The park is laid out as a series of formal terraces, and there are plenty of benches, which are popular both summer and winter. It also includes an open-air café, a puppet theatre and a bandstand. There are even some tennis courts.

Located in the north-eastern corner of the gardens is the **Fontaine de Medicis**. Built in the style of an Italian grotto, it was designed by Nicolas de Brosses in 1620 for Marie de Medicis and is a stunning Baroque fountain standing at the end of a narrow shady pool. It moved to its present location in 1860, and the mythological figures were added by August Ottin in 1866 – Polyphemus seen hovering threateningly over the beautifully rendered figures of Acis and Galatea, these are in turn flanked by Pan and Diana.

The **Palais du Luxembourg** is home to the French Senate. Originally a town house built by Alexandre de la Tourette in 1564, it occupied the site of an old Roman camp. It then became the property of the duc de Luxembourg who sold it to Marie de Medicis, widow of Henri IV, in 1612. The Queen

Luxembourg

Palais du Luxembourg

commissioned Salomon de Brosse to design her a home based on the Pitti Palace in Florence. She was able to move in with her two sons, Louis XIII and Gaston Duc d'Orléans, in 1625, even though the palace wasn't fully completed until 1631. Shortly after it was finished, the Queen was forced into exile after having attempted an abortive coup. The Queen left the palace to her second and favourite son, Gaston, in 1642. It remained a royal palace until the Revolution and was open two days a week as a museum between 1750 and 1779.

During the Revolution it was briefly used as a prison and then later served as the first residence of the Emperor Napoleon. It became home to the senate in 1800. It was extensively altered in the 19th century, with a new garden façade being built by Alphonse de Gisors. It acted as the Luftwaffe's

headquarters during World War II, when air-raid shelters were built under the gardens. Symmetrically arranged around a courtyard which opens out through a triumphal entranceway topped by a dome, its east gallery houses the Musée du Luxembourg. The Orangerie, located in the private garden of the Petit Luxembourg, is the home of the President of the Senate.

Did You Know?

The Jardin du Luxembourg lies on a north-south axis with the Observatoire de Paris. This lines up with the meridian of Paris, which is slightly to the east of the garden's central fountain, and is marked by a small plaque in the pavement where the low stone balustrade in front of the palace begins to curve.

Luxembourg

Jardin du Luxembourg
Opening times: Dawn to dusk daily
Tel: 01. 42 34 23 89

Palais du Luxembourg
Opening times: One Sat per month
Website: www.senat.fr
Tel: 01. 42 34 20 60 (groups) 01. 44 54 19 49 (individuals)

St-Sulpice ❼

Exit the Jardin du Luxembourg via rue de Vaugirard and turn left. Follow it until you come to rue Férou and turn right. St-Sulpice will be ahead of you on your right. This elegant Neoclassical church is the second building on this site, having replaced a Romanesque place of worship dating from the 13th century. This newer church was begun in 1646 and construction lasted about 140 years. The chancel is the work of Louis Le Vau and others, while the

St-Sulpice

construction was actually completed by a student of François Mansart, Gilles-Marie Oppenord. Dedicated to Sulpitius the Pious, the church is only slightly smaller than Notre-Dame.

The church's beautiful façade is by Giovanni Niccolo Servandoni and dates from 1732. It is an unusually restrained piece of Neoclassicism in an era famous for its riotous Rococo. Consisting of two tiers of columns with loggias behind them, the only jarring note is the fact that the two towers don't quite match. Jean Francois Chalgrin altered one of them just before the Revolution, and the other one has been left untouched ever since. The church was turned into a Temple of Victory during the Revolution, when its interior was damaged. This was repaired by hiring Eugène Delacroix to paint some magnificent murals in the 19th century. These murals adorn the side chapel and are *Jacob Wrestling with the Angel*, *Heliodorus Driven from the Temple* and *St Michael Killing the Dragon*.

Place St-Sulpice, the large square in front of the church, was built in the second half of the 18th century and its main feature is the **Fontaine des Quatres Points Cardinaux** (Fountain of the Four Cardinal Points) by Joachim Visconti and dating from 1844. Depicting four French church leaders facing in the direction of the four cardinal points, the fountain's name is also a pun – *point* also means 'never' in French, which means that these four leaders never got to the rank of cardinal. Overlooking the square is the **Café de la Mairie**, a popular spot with students and writers, and frequently seen in French films.

St-Sulpice

Opening times: 7.30am–7.30pm daily
Tel: 01. 42 34 59 98

Did You Know?
The Marquis de Sade and Charles Baudelaire were both baptised at St-Sulpice.

St-Joseph-des-Carmes ❽

Retrace your steps back to rue de Vaugirard and turn right. The church of St-Joseph-des-Carmes will be on your right at No. 70. This simple little church faces out onto a small courtyard and was built as a chapel for a Carmelite convent in 1620. Used as a prison during the Revolution, more than 100 priests met an untimely death here in the church's courtyard during the September Massacres of 1792. Their remains are now buried in the crypt.

St-Joseph-des-Carmes

Opening times: 7am–7pm Mon–Sat; 9am–7pm Sun
Closed Easter Mon, Pentecost
Tel: 01. 44 39 52 00

Luxembourg

St-Joseph-des-Carmes

Institute Catholique de Paris ❾

Around the corner to the right from St-Joseph-des-Carmes is the Institute Catholique de Paris, at No. 21 rue d'Assas. This is one of the most distinguished teaching institutions in France. It was founded in 1875 and has approximately 23,000 students. It is also home to a small museum, the Musée Biblique (Biblical Museum), which shows objects that have been excavated in the Holy Land, giving an interesting insight into the daily life of ancient Palestine.

Institute Catholique de Paris
Website: www.icp.fr
Tel: 01. 44 39 52 00

Musée Biblique
Opening times: 4–6pm Sat or by appointment
Tel: 01. 45 48 09 15

Link to the Montparnasse walk: Continue along rue de Vaugirard and turn left onto Boulevard Raspail.

Montparnasse

Nearest Metro: Vavin
Approximate walking time: 2 hours

Montparnasse

Named after the mountain sacred to the Greek god Apollo – god of poetry, music and beauty – Mount Parnassus was also the abode of the muses, which makes it a particularly appropriate name for this part of the city. Home to some of the 19th and 20th centuries' most important artistic creators, Montparnasse was where Picasso and Modigliani had their studios, as well as Bourdelle and Zadkine, names somewhat less known now but who were famous in their day. The lower rents of this unfashionable part of the city attracted struggling young artists and writers. Cocteau, Giacometti, Hemingway, Matisse and Modigliani could all be seen in the bars and cafés of Montparnasse in the first decades of the 20th century. The area is also famous for its cemetery, and its catacombs and of course the Tour Montparnasse, the tallest building in France.

THE WALK

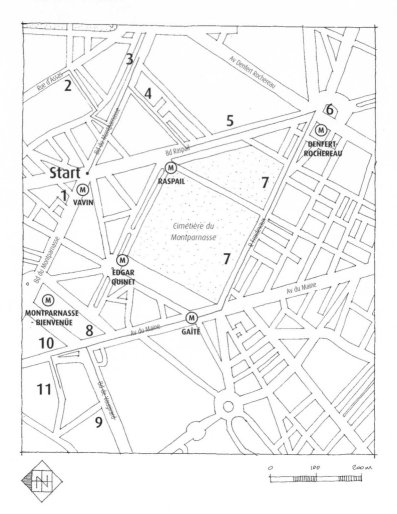

KEY

Montparnasse

La Coupole ❶

Exit the Vavin metro station and you will see La Coupole at No. 102 Boulevard du Montparnasse. This historic restaurant, café and dance hall was founded in 1927 and underwent a major face-lift in the 1980s. Its patrons included Josephine Baker, Jean-Paul Sartre and, more recently, Roman Polanski. Its famous columns, decorated by local artists, can still be seen. Legend has it that they were painted by people who couldn't afford their bills, but actually the café owners asked some local artists to decorate them in exchange for all the alcohol they could drink.

Rodin's famous **statue of Balzac** stands at the junction of Boulevard du Montparnasse and Boulevard Raspail. Erected in 1939, it stands 3 metres (10 feet) tall and caused a scandal when it was unveiled because it portrayed the writer in his dressing gown (his usual mode of attire for creative endeavour), which was considered too unseemly for public view.

La Coupole
Opening times: 8pm–1am Mon–Thur, 8.30pm–1.30am Fri–Sun
Website: www.flobrasseries.com
Tel: 01. 43 20 14 20

Musée Zadkine ❷

Walk along Boulevard du Montparnasse and turn left at rue Paul Séjourné, then take a right onto rue Notre-Dame-des-Champs and immediately left onto rue Joseph Bara. At the end of this street you will come to rue d'Assas and the Musée Zadkine will be on your left at No. 100 bis. This one-man museum, in the former home of Russian-born sculptor Ossip Zadkine, is well worth a visit. Although less well known these days, he has done some important work, including two monuments to van Gogh, one for the Netherlands and another for Auvers-sur-Oise, where the famous Dutch artist died.

Musée Zadkine

Zadkine also produced the powerful *Ville Détruite*, a powerful sculpture commissioned by Rotterdam after its destruction in World War II. The sculptor lived in this house from 1928 until his death in 1967 and the museum's exhibits show the development of his work, from Cubist beginnings to the more individual Abstract-Expressionist style that became his trademark.

Musée Zadkine
Opening times: 10am–6pm Tue–Sun
Closed public hols
Website: www.zadkine.paris.fr
Tel: 01. 55 42 77 20

La Closerie des Lilas ❸

Retrace your steps to Boulevard du Montparnasse and turn left. La Closerie des Lilas will be on your left at No. 171. This was the favourite bar of writers like Hemingway and Scott Fitzgerald as well as revolutionaries such as Lenin and Trotsky. The décor has remained unchanged since those glory days, and the terrace is still popular. Hemingway is reputed to have written most of *The Sun Also Rises* on the terrace in just six weeks.

La Closerie des Lilas
Opening times:
Bar: 11–2am daily
Brasserie: noon–1am daily
Website: www.closeriedeslilas.fr
Tel: 01. 40 51 34 50

Rue Campagne-Première ❹

Walk back up Boulevard du Montparnasse a little and turn left onto rue Campagne-Première. This street has some interesting Art Nouveau buildings, particularly the row of artists' studios on the left at No. 31. Overlooking the small park, these were built in 1911 and the building's façade was decorated by the ceramicist Paul Bigot. Between World Wars I and II many famous artists lived and worked here, including Picasso, Joan Miró and Kandinsky. Modigliani, ravaged by opium and tuberculosis, spent the last years of his life at No. 3.

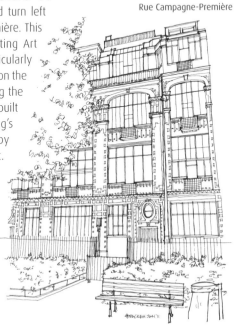

Rue Campagne-Première

Montparnasse

Fondation Cartier ⑤

Walk to the end of rue Campagne-Première and turn left onto Boulevard Raspail. The Fondation Cartier will be on your left at No. 261. An elegantly simple building, it was designed by French architect Jean Nouvel to house this contemporary art foundation. The structure has a lightness and transparency that acts as the perfect foil to the progressive works of art on show. Some of the exhibitions also showcase individual, group or thematic displays, often featuring work by new young artists. The complex incorporates a magnificent cedar of Lebanon, which was planted by François-René de Chateaubriand in 1823.

Fondation Cartier
Opening times: 11am–8pm Tue–Sun (until 10pm Thur)
Closed 1 Jan, 25 Dec
Website: www.foundation.cartier.fr
Tel: 01. 42 18 56 50

Catacombes ⑥

Continue along Boulevard Raspail until you come to Denfert Rochereau. The entrance to the Paris Catacombes is at No. 1 Avenue du Colonel Henri Rol-Tanguy. Over the entrance to this vast network of underground tunnels is written: 'Stop! This is the empire of death'. This strange place was the result of a 1786 plan to move the millions of skeletons from the city-centre cemeteries in places like Les Halles to a number of unused quarries at Paris' three 'mountains': Montparnasse, Montrouge and Montsouris. It took 15 months to transport all the skulls and bones, and not a few rotting corpses, across the city. This was done at night, so as not to offend the sensibilities of the population. Huge carts could be seen rumbling across the city night after night, carrying their macabre cargo. Just before the Revolution, the Compte d'Artois (who was later King Charles X) used to throw wild parties here, while during World War II the French Resistance set up its headquarters in these vast and secretive tunnels.

Lion, Denfert Rochereau

Catacombes
Opening times: 10am–5pm Tue–Sun (last admission 4pm)
Closed public hols
Website: www.carnavalet.paris.fr
Tel: 01. 43 22 47 63

Cimetière du Montparnasse ❼

Walk up rue Froidevaux and the Cimetière du Montparnasse will be on your right. It is one of a number of cemeteries planned outside the city walls by Napoleon to replace the small, unsanitary cemeteries in the city, which were increasingly seen as a health hazard in the 19th century. It opened in 1824 and is, like most French cemeteries, divided into neatly arranged blocks connected by paths crossing at right angles.

Cimetière du Montparnasse with
Tour Montparnasse

Montparnasse

Rue Emile Richard cuts the cemetery in two, with the Petit Cimetière on the street's eastern side and the Grand Cimetière on the west. Horace Daillon's lovely sculpture, the Génie du Sommeil Eternel (Spirit of Eternal Sleep), dates back to 1902 and stands at one of the more important cemetery crossings; while the remains of a 17th-century windmill overlook the Allee Raffet. This was formerly part of the Brothers of Charity monastery, on which the cemetery was built. Brancusi's *Kiss*, a Cubist *hommage* to Rodin's statue of the same name, stands at the southern end of the rue Emile Richard.

Many famous French men and women are buried here, including Alfred Dreyfus, the Jewish army officer whose trumped-up trial for treason in 1894 provoked the international scandal known as the Dreyfus Affair. Other somewhat happier figures include that of the mid-20th-century power couple Jean-Paul Sartre and Simone de Beauvoir, the composers Camille Saint-Saëns and Serge Gainsbourg, writers Guy de Maupassant and Charles Baudelaire, and the industrialist André Citroën (founder of the famous car company). Charles Pigeon, also an industrialist, is now more famous for his flamboyant tomb, which depicts him in bed with his wife. Frédéric Auguste Bartholdi, the sculptor of New York's Statue of Liberty in 1886, is also buried here. Famous foreigners include Irish playwright Samuel Beckett, American actress Jean Seberg and the American photographer Man Ray, who did much to immortalise the cultural life of Montparnasse in the 1920s and '30s.

Cimetière du Montparnasse

Opening times: 8am–6pm daily (from 8.30am Sat, from 9am Sun), mid-Mar–early Nov; closes at 5.30pm early Nov–mid-Mar
Tel: 01. 44 10 86 50

Tour Montparnasse 8

Continue up rue Froidevaux and turn right onto Avenue du Maine. Tour Montparnasse will be on your right at Place Raoul Dautry. This massive office tower, the tallest building in France, and the ninth tallest in the European Union, was built between 1969 and 1972 as the focal point of a new business district for the city. It was Europe's largest office block at the time. Standing 210 metres (690 feet) tall, it totally dominates the city's southern skyline, and the views from the top floor, the 59th, are spectacular – up to 40 kilometres (25 miles) on a clear day.

Officially called Tour Maine-Montparnasse, the building stands on 56 piles that extend 62 metres (203 feet) below ground and boasts the fastest lift in Europe (travelling 56 floors in 38 seconds). The tower also contains a restaurant with wonderful views. Designed by architects Eugène Beaudouin, Urbain Cassan and Louis Hoym de Marien, its elegantly curved façade has allowed the tower to age more gracefully than many of its contemporaries.

Tour Montparnasse

Opening times:
9.30am–11.30pm daily (last lift 11pm), Apr–Sept;
9.30am–10.30pm daily (to 11pm Fri and Sat), Oct–Mar
Website: www.tourmontparnasse56.com
Tel: 01. 45 38 52 56

Musée de la Poste ❾

Turn left onto Boulevard de Vaugirard and the Musée de la Poste will be on your right at No. 34. This small but interesting museum covers every aspect of the French postal service, including well-laid-out displays of postage-stamp art and the numerous methods of delivery. There is even a room dedicated to how post was delivered in times of war, it shows how carrier pigeons used to deliver letters during the Franco-Prussian War – they had postmarks stamped onto their wings.

Musée de la Poste

Opening times: 10am–6pm Mon–Sat
Closed public hols
Website: www.museedelaposte.fr
Tel: 01. 42 79 23 00

Musée du Montparnasse ❿

Return to Avenue du Maine and turn left. The Musée du Montparnasse will be on your right at No. 21. This delightful little museum opened in 1998 in the former studio of Russian-born artist Marie Vassilieff, who lived here in the early 20th century. The museum was founded by Roger Pic and Jean-Marie Drot as a non-profit organisation and highlights the area's rich artistic tradition. It also hosts temporary exhibitions of Montparnasse artists, past and present.

Up to and during World War I, Marie Vassilieff operated what was registered as a private club; it acted as a canteen for the area's many needy artists so they could eat and drink cheaply, which kept many of them going, including the likes of Picasso and Modigliani. The canteen soon gained a reputation as a breeding ground for new ideas, and Fernand Léger even gave a number of lectures on Modern art here in 1913. The museum hosts monthly meetings and cultural events as part of its membership programme.

Musée du Montparnasse

Opening times: 12.30–7pm Tue–Sun
Website: www.museedumontparnasse.net
Tel: 01. 42 22 91 96

Montparnasse

Musée Antoine Bourdelle ⓫

Almost opposite the Musée du Montparnasse is the entrance to rue Antoine Bourdelle. The Musée Antoine Bourdelle will be on the right-hand side at No. 18. This red-brick building was designed in 1992 by Christian de Portzamparc and houses the museum dedicated to the sculptor Antoine Bourdelle as well as the symbolist painter Eugène Carrière.

Located in Bourdelle's former studio, which is where he lived from 1884 until his death in 1929, it contains an excellent overview of this formerly popular artist's work. About 900 works are on display, including the original plaster casts for monumental public works that now grace many a Paris square. Bourdelle, although no longer so well known, was one of France's best-known sculptors around the turn of the 20th century. He had also worked as an assistant to Rodin, who admired his work. The museum hosts temporary exhibitions from time to time.

Musée Antoine Bourdelle
Opening times: 10am–6pm Tue–Sun
Closed public hols
Website: www.bourdelle.paris.fr
Tel: 01. 49 54 73 73

Link to the Invalides walk: Return to Avenue du Maine and turn left. Turn left again onto Boulevard du Montparnasse and follow it as it turns into Boulevard des Invalides.

Invalides

Nearest Metro: St-François-Xavier
Approximate walking time: 2 hours

Invalides

This is one of the most spectacular parts of Paris, home to the iconic Eiffel Tower, the Ecole Militaire and the Champ-de-Mars, the beautiful park that connects them. The area takes its name from the impressive Hôtel des Invalides, which was built by Louis XIV for wounded soldiers, and has at its focal point the magnificent gilded Dôme, the Sun King's personal church, which also houses the tomb of Napoleon. Invalides is full of excellent museums, including the Musée Rodin, Musée Maillol and the Musée du Quai Branly. This has long been one of the smartest parts of the city and home to aristocratic town houses, many of which are now embassies, with one in particular, the beautiful Hôtel Matignon, the official residence of French prime ministers. The area has a more down-to-earth side as well, with the lively street market on rue Cler and the Paris sewers (Les Égouts), the entrance to which is on Quai d'Orsay.

THE WALK

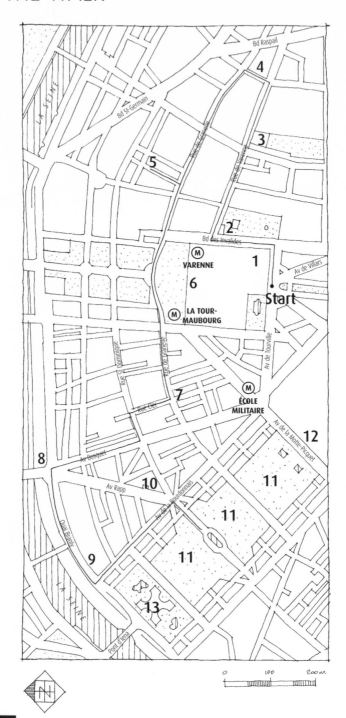

Bd Raspail

4

Bd St-Germain

3

Rue de Grenelle

Rue de Bellechasse

5

2

Bd des Invalides

(M) VARENNE

1

Av de Villars

6

Start

(M) LA TOUR-
MAUBOURG

Av de Tourville

Rue St-Dominique

Rue de Grenelle

7

(M) ÉCOLE
MILITAIRE

Rue Cler

12

Av de la Motte-Picquet

8

Av Bosquet

11

Av Rapp

10

11

Av de la Bourdonnais

Quai Branly

11

9

LA SEINE

13

Pont d'Iéna

0   100   200 m

N

KEY

Invalides

Dôme

Dôme ❶

Leave the St-François-Xavier metro station and walk up Avenue de Villars. The Dôme will be straight ahead of you. A soldiers' church already stood here when Louis XIV asked Jules Hardouin-Mansart to build this magnificent structure as his personal chapel in 1676. It was to be reserved for the exclusive use of the King and to act as the place for royal tombs. The tombs never materialised, but this spectacular example of Baroque architecture still remains a monument to Bourbon glory. The church itself took 27 years to build, and the dome (107 metres or 350 feet) occupies half of its height and dominates the rest of the building with its fine proportioning. First gilded in 1715, it was regilded in 1937 and again in 1989.

The interior ceiling of the Dôme contains a painting by Charles de la Fosse, the *Glory of Paradise*. Dating from 1692, it shows St-Louis presenting his sword to Christ. Napoleon's final wish was to 'rest on the banks of the Seine', so in 1840 King Louis-Philippe decided to bring the Emperor's body back from St Helena. This was seen as a gesture of goodwill to his Republican and

Bonapartist opponents. The Dôme, which was near the river, and had military and royal associations, was thought the ideal choice for the Emperor's tomb. However, it wasn't until 1861 that Napoleon's body was finally interred here, in the glass-topped crypt. This was done in a solemn ceremony attended by Napoleon's nephew, the new Emperor Napoleon III. Access to the crypt is via a curved staircase in front of the altar. The tombs of two of Napoleon's brothers are also to be found in this church: Joseph Bonaparte, Napoleon's older brother (who was the King of Naples and, later, Spain), is in one of the side chapels near the main entrance, while their younger brother, Jérôme, King of Westphalia, lies in St Jérôme's Chapel.

The church is also home to the tomb of Marshal Foch, with an imposing bronze memorial built in 1937 by Paul Landowski. There is also a touching memorial to the great military architect and engineer Sébastian le Prestre de Vauban. This was commissioned by Napoleon in 1808. Vauban worked for Louis XIV and died in 1707. He revolutionised siege warfare by introducing the ricochet-battery, a type of fortification system. His tomb, which contains his heart, features a reclining figure mourned by science and war, and was executed by Antoine Etex.

Dôme
Opening times: 10am–5pm daily (mid-Jan–mid-Sept 7pm)
Closed first Mon of the month, 1 Jan, 1 May, 1 Nov, 25 Dec
Tel: 01. 44 42 38 77

Musée Rodin ❷

Walk up Boulevard des Invalides, away from Avenue de Tourville, and turn right onto rue de Varenne. The Musée Rodin will be on your right at No. 77. Auguste Rodin is widely regarded as one of France's greatest sculptors. He revolutionised the art of sculpture in the 19th century and this beautiful 18th-century mansion, the Hôtel Biron, is where he lived and worked from 1908 until his death in 1917. In return for the use of this state-owned property, Rodin left his work to the nation. It is now housed in a series of exhibits arranged chronologically and spanning the whole of his remarkable career. It includes such masterpieces as *The Kiss* and *Eve*. Some of his sculptures are also on display in the garden, including *The Burghers of Calais, The Thinker* and *Balzac*.

Musée Rodin
Opening times: 9.30am–5.45pm Tue–Sun, Apr–Sept; 9.30am–4.45pm Tue–Sun (garden one hour later), Oct–Mar
Closed 1 Jan, 1 May, 25 Dec
Website: www.musee-rodin.fr
Tel: 01. 44 18 61 10

Invalides

Hôtel Matignon ❸

Continue along rue de Varenne and you will come to the Hôtel Matignon on your right at No. 57. This building is one of the most beautiful houses in Paris, and has a long and fascinating history. Since 1958 it has been the official residence of the prime ministers of France, it also has the largest private garden in the city. The building was built by architect Jean Courtonne in 1722 for a Marshal of France called the Prince de Tigny, who wanted to create a country estate in this as yet undeveloped part of Paris. However, the building cost so much that the Prince was obliged to sell it and the Compte de Matignon bought it for his son.

The richly-decorated interior by Michel Lange, Jean-Martin Pelletier and Jean Herpin was much admired, and the owners even allowed any 'well-dressed' person to come in and inspect it while they were away. In 1731 the wife of Jacques de Matignon, who was a Grimaldi, succeeded her father as head of the principality of Monaco. Her son then became Prince Honoré III of Monaco in 1734. He was imprisoned during the Revolution but managed to keep his head, no doubt due to his well-known revolutionary sympathies. He was penniless when released in 1794, however, and the property was put under seal. His sons obtained its release and sold it in 1802 to Anne Eleonore Franchi, a professional dancer. She was the mistress of, among others, the Duke of Wurttemberg and the Emperor Joseph II of Austria. Maria-Theresa had her banished from Austria as soon as she came to the throne, so Anne Eleonore found herself in the West Indies of all places, where she met the wealthy Scottish banker Quentin Crawford, and together they refurbished the house.

In 1808, it passed into the hands of politician Charles Maurice de Talleyrand-Périgord, who founded a salon. Financial misdealing obliged him to sell the building and Napoleon bought it in 1811. After the Bourbon restoration in 1814, Louis XVIII swapped the house for the Elysées Palace. The Duchesse de Bourbon who took it over established a community of nuns here, which her niece moved to the Rue de Picpus when she inherited the building, and rented it out. A wealthy American called Colonel Thorn used the mansion as his base for launching his children into European society – and they all made brilliant marriages – but the revolution of 1848 obliged the Colonel to return to New York.

The hotel was then sold to the Duke of Galliera (whose wife was a niece of the Princess of Monaco). They were one of the richest couples in Europe and in 1870, at the Duchess' suggestion, the Compte de Paris (the main Pretender to the French throne) moved into the ground floor. At a party given in 1886 to celebrate the Compte's daughter's marriage to Carlos, heir to the Portuguese throne, so many monarchists descended on the capital that the government got nervous and passed a law within a week that exiled them from the city. The Duchess was displeased at this and also moved away. She willed the house to the Austro-Hungarian Emperor, who turned it into an embassy. But World War I saw France at war with Austria and the mansion was declared enemy property, only to become French property once again after prolonged negotiations in 1922. It was on the point of being divided up into flats when it was saved and turned into the headquarters of the President of the Council, the Third Republic's head of government, a title which changed to prime minister in 1958.

Musée Maillol ❹

Continue along rue de Varenne and turn left at rue du Bac and then right onto rue de Grenelle. The Musée Maillol will be on your right at No. 61. Large statues representing the city of Paris and the four seasons adorn Bouchardon's fountain in front of this house, which was the home of the novelist Alfred de Musset. Turned into the Musée Maillol by Dina Vierny in 1995, a former model of the artist, all aspects of Aristide Maillol's work can be seen here. This includes paintings and sculpture as well as engravings, drawings and *objets d'art*. Dina Vierny's was also a discerning collector in her own right, and the museum contains works by, among others, Matisse, Cézanne, Degas, Picasso and Ingres.

Musée Maillol
Opening times: 11am–6pm Wed–Mon
(last admission 5.15pm)
Closed public hols
Website: www.museemaillol.com
Tel: 01. 42 22 59 58

Musée Maillol

Invalides

Ste-Clotilde ❺

Retrace your steps along rue de Grenelle and follow it until you come to rue de Martignac. Sainte-Clotilde will be ahead of you on your right. This imposing Gothic style basilica was designed by German-born architect François-Christian Gau and was the first building to be built in this style in the city since the Middle Ages. Named after the second wife of the Frankish King Clovis, who lived from 475 to 545, the church was first planned by the Paris City Council in 1827, but it was 1846 before construction began. Gau died in 1853 and the work was continued by Theodore Ballu. It opened in 1857 and was declared a basilica by Pope Leo XIII in 1896. The imposing twin steeples can be seen from across the Seine, while the church's interior contains stations of the cross sculpted by James Pradier and some rich stained-glass windows depicting scenes from the life of Sainte Clotilde. The well-known composer César Franck was church organist here for more than 30 years from 1859.

Ste-Clotilde
Opening times: 9am–7pm daily
Closed non-religious public hols
Website: www.sainte-clothilde.com
Tel: 01. 44 18 62 60

Sainte-Clotilde

Hôtel des Invalides ❻

Return to rue de Grenelle and turn right. The Hôtel des Invalides will be on your left, centred on the great axis leading to the river. The restrained Neoclassical façade of this building is one of the most impressive sights in Paris, particularly when seen from Pont Alexandre III. It was founded as a military hospital and retirement home for French veterans by Louis XIV in 1670. Until then soldiers who had been disabled by war had to beg on the street. The building is still a veterans' hospital today.

Construction lasted five years, and was based on designs by Libéral Bruand. The complex houses a number of military museums, with the south side of it abutting St-Louis-des-Invalides, the soldiers' church, which backs onto the magnificent Dôme. The Cour d'Honneur is still used for military parades, and there is a statue of Napoleon by Seurre on its south side. The formal tree-lined gardens, which stretch all the way down to the Seine, were laid out by de Cotte in 1704 and are lined with bronze cannons dating from the 17th and 18th centuries.

The entrance to the **Musée de l'Ordre de la Libération** is at No. 51 bis Boulevard de la Tour-Maubourg. This museum highlights the struggle of the Free French during World War II, who resisted and eventually managed to overthrow the Germans occupying their country. The Order of Liberation was created by General Charles de Gaulle in 1940 and bestowed on anyone who had made an outstanding contribution towards that final victory. It is France's highest honour and was given to members of the French armed forces, civilians, as well as a number of important allies, including King George VI, Winston Churchill and General Eisenhower.

The **Musée de l'Armée** is one of the most comprehensive museums of military history in the world. Its exhibits include Stone Age weapons as well as those used in World War II. It is also home to the third-largest collection of armour in the world. The Ancient Armoury is located in the old refectory and is full of interesting displays. It also boasts some 17th-century murals which, thanks to a recent restoration, are visible for the first time in two centuries. Painted by Joseph Parrocel, they celebrate a number of Louis XIV's military victories. The **Cour de Valeur** contains an educational display highlighting the life of General de Gaulle.

The **Musée des Plans-Reliefs** is home to detailed models of French fortifications, some of which date back to the reign of Louis XIV. The oldest is that of the fortified town of Perpignan, which is from 1686. This was designed by the famous 17th-century military architect and engineer Sébastien Le Prestre de Vauban, who was responsible for many of the defences around French towns, including Briançon. The museum also contains a display on model-making.

The chapel of **St-Louis-des-Invalides**, also known as the soldiers' church, was built by Jules Hardouin-Mansart between 1679 and 1708. It was based on an original design by Libéral Bruand. This stark interior is enlivened by banners seized in battle. The fine organ was built by Alexandre Thierry in the 17th-century and was where Berlioz's *Requiem* was premiered in 1837, with an orchestra consisting of a battery of artillery outside.

Hôtel des Invalides
Opening times: 10am–6pm daily (5pm winter)
Closed 1 Jan, 1 May, 1 Nov, 25 Dec
Website: www.invalides.org
Tel: 01. 44 42 38 77

Musée de l'Ordre de la Libération
Opening times: 10am–6pm daily (6.30pm Sun), Apr–Sept;
10am–5pm daily (5.30pm Sun), Oct-Mar
Tel: 01. 47 05 04 10

Musée de l'Armée
Opening times: 10am–6pm daily (5pm Oct–Mar), last admission 45 mins before closing
Closed first Mon of the month (unless a bank hol), 1 Jan, 1 May, 1 Nov, 25 Dec
Ticket includes entry to the Musée de l'Ordre de la Libération and the Musée des Plans-Reliefs
Website: www.invalides.org
Tel: 01. 44 42 38 77

Musée des Plans-Reliefs
Opening times: 10am–6pm daily (5pm Oct–Mar)
Closed first Mon of the month, 1 Jan, 1 May, 1 and 11 Nov, 25 Dec
Tel: 01. 45 51 95 05

St-Louis-des-Invalides
Opening times: 10am–5.30pm daily, Apr–Sept; 10am–4.30pm daily, Oct–Mar
Tel: 01. 44 42 37 65

Did You Know?
Many of the models on display at the Musée des Plans-Reliefs were considered to be top secret until as late as the 1950s.

Rue Cler ❼

Continue along rue de Grenelle and you will come to rue Cler. This is one of the most up-market street markets in the city. Located in the heart of the 7th arondissement, one of the city's wealthiest areas, it is home to well-to-do professionals and a number of embassies and as such attracts a clientele that can afford to pay that little bit more. This colourful market occupies a pedestrian street that runs south from rue de Grenelle. Home to excellent shops and stalls, the produce is top quality, with the patisseries and cheese shops being particularly good.

Rue Cler
Market Tue–Sat

Les Égouts de Paris ❽

Exit rue Cler via rue St-Dominique, then take a right onto Avenue Bosquet and the entrance to Les Égouts de Paris will be at the top of the avenue overlooking the river (opposite No. 93 Quai d'Orsay). This is a popular if somewhat eccentric tourist attraction. Baron Haussmann is most famous for the grand boulevards he built throughout the city in the mid-19th century, but one of his most important achievements was Paris' sewerage system (*égouts*). This museum explains their history and workings and makes for an interesting if unusual visit. Tours are limited to the small part of the sewer network around the Quai d'Orsay, which is just as well, as they stretch more than 2,100 kilometres (1,300 miles) under the city.

Les Égouts de Paris
Opening times: 11am–5pm Sat–Wed (to 4pm in winter)
Closed two weeks in Jan
Tel: 01. 53 68 27 81

Musée du Quai Branly ❾

Walk along Quai Branly and you will come to the Musée du Quai Branly on your left. This remarkable museum by architect Jean Nouvel displays 3,500 exhibits from the French state's collection of non-Western art. Established by former President Jacques Chirac, this popular museum opened in 2006. Perched on pillars above a lush garden, a group of four inter-connected buildings made of glass, wood and concrete are organised around symbols of forests, rivers and, oddly, death and oblivion. Tickets are purchased outside the main building, and once inside visitors follow a 180-metre (590-foot) ramp that spirals around a glass tower displaying musical instruments. This leads to the main collections, from which routes pass through four colour-coded zones dedicated to Oceania, Asia, Africa and the Americas. There are stairs to three mezzanine galleries, one of which is home to the museum's multimedia resources. There is also a rooftop restaurant with stunning views in the garden, which is home to 15,000 carefully tended plants, and a 500-seat auditorium used for open-air music and dance performances.

Musée du Quai Branly
Opening times: 11am–7pm daily (9pm Thur–Sat)
Website: www.quaibranly.fr
Tel: 01. 56 61 70 00

Invalides

No. 29 Avenue Rapp ❿

Turn left onto Avenue de la Bourdonnais and where this avenue meets Avenue Rapp you will be able to see the remarkable Art Nouveau apartment building at No. 29. This is one of the most famous examples of Art Nouveau in the city. Designed by Jules Lavirotte, it won first prize at the Concours des Facades de la Ville de Paris in 1901. Its ceramic tiles and brickwork are decorated with numerous undulating animal and flower motifs that intermingle with sultry female figures. Deliberately erotic, these were considered quite subversive in their day. Also worth a visit is another Lavirotte building that sits on nearby Square Rapp, which sports a watchtower.

No. 29 Avenue Rapp

Champ-de-Mars ⓫

These gardens stretch from the Eiffel Tower to the Ecole Militaire and were originally a parade ground for the cadets at the military academy. This vast formal park is a sort of melange of French and English garden design – the central part with its regularly gridded beds and paths is French, and the sides are laid out in the more undulating English style. It forms part of one of the most striking and famous perspectives in the city: the axis from the Ecole Militaire to the Eiffel Tower and the Palais de Chaillot on the other side of the river. It started out as a military parade ground, hence its name, the Field of Mars, and was reduced to its present size of 24 hectares (60 acres) in 1928. The area is a popular place to celebrate Bastille Day, with the first such celebration being held here in 1790. One of its spectators was the former King Louis XVI, known as Citizen Capet, there as a sort of guest of dishonour. The Champ-de-Mars has also been used for horse-racing, balloon ascents and World Expositions, including the famous one in 1889 which saw the erection of the Eiffel Tower.

Ecole Militaire ⓬

Designed by architect Jacques-Ange Gabriel, this is a simple essay in stark, symmetrical Neoclassicism, although the interior is in a more lavish Louis XVI style. The central pavilion of this royal military academy, which was founded by Louis XV in 1751 to educate the sons of impoverished officers, features eight Corinthian pillars under a quadrangular dome. The chapel is particularly beautiful, as is the central staircase, which features a decorative wrought-iron banister designed by Gabriel.

Ecole Militaire
Visits by special permission only, contact the commandant in writing.

Did You Know?
Napoleon was a cadet at the Ecole Militaire, and on passing out his report rather presciently observed that 'he could go far if the circumstances are right'.

Ecole Militaire

Eiffel Tower ⓭

Built as part of the Universal Exposition held in Paris in 1889, the Eiffel Tower was only meant to be a temporary structure. Designed by the engineer Gustave Eiffel, who had built a number of iron railway bridges in Europe and South

America, it stands at a height of 324 metres (1,062 feet) and was the world's tallest building until the Empire State Building was completed in New York in 1931. The Tower has become the symbol of Paris, yet when it was first built it was fiercely criticised for being too ugly.

Constructed between January 1887 and March 1889, it contains 15,000 different parts held together by up to 2.5 million rivets and weighs 7,000 tonnes. A brilliant feat of engineering, it was assembled out of relatively small parts, which together form a strong, lightweight and wind-resistant whole. Eiffel's genius was to give it its unforgettable profile, a design which was the result of an aesthetic rather than technical requirement – the sweeping arches that connect the feet of the tower appear to carry its weight but are in fact decorative, they hang from the superstructure. The entire structure takes 18 months to paint and this is done every five or ten years. Recently renovated, it now sports a dazzling 10-minute light show every evening on the hour.

The first level, at 57 metres (187 feet), can be reached by lift or 360 steps and is where the Cineffel is located, a small museum dedicated to the history of the tower. A short film shows footage of famous visitors, including Charlie Chaplin and Adolf Hitler. There is also a post office. The second level, at 115 metres (376 feet), is a further 359 steps higher and can also be reached by lift. The Le Jules Verne Restaurant is located here and commands magnificent views of the city. The third level is at 276 metres (905 feet) while the top, the antennae, is at 324 metres (1,062 feet). From the Viewing Gallery it is possible to see up to 70 kilometres (45 miles) away. The lifts are double-decker and were installed as a hydraulic system in 1900, they were automated in 1986. There is also a bust of Gustave Eiffel by Antoine Bourdelle underneath the tower, placed there in 1929.

Eiffel Tower
Opening times: 9.30am–11.45pm daily (6.30pm for stairs), Sept–mid-Jun; 9am–0.45am daily (last admission one hour before), mid-Jun–Aug
Website: www.tour-eiffel.fr
Tel: 01. 44 11 23 23

Did You Know?
The Eiffel Tower was only intended to be a temporary structure, the fact that it was a convenient place for a radio mast saved it from destruction in 1898.

Did You Know?
The writer Guy de Maupassant hated the sight of the Eiffel Tower, yet he lunched there every day, saying that it was the only place in the city where he couldn't see it.

Link to the Trocadéro walk: Cross Pont d'Iéna and turn left onto Avenue du Président Kennedy.

Trocadéro

Nearest Metro: Passy
Approximate walking time: 1 hour 30 minutes

Trocadéro

This part of Paris, centred on the Place du Trocadéro, is one of the most exclusive areas in the city. It is also known as Chaillot, a name which comes from the village that used to stand here and that got swallowed up by Paris in the 19th century. It was transformed into grand avenues and noble mansions and is popular with embassies. The area is also well known for its cafés and restaurants, and has some of the city's most fascinating museums, covering Asian art, contemporary art and fashion. In fact, Avenue du Président Wilson has the highest concentration of museums of any street in the city. Standing at the heart of the district are the sweeping, symmetrical wings of the Palais de Chaillot, which act as the imposing western end of the axis running from the Ecole Militaire through the Eiffel Tower. The Palais' hilly position allows it magnificent panoramas of this part of the city and it is also one of the best places from which to photograph the Eiffel Tower.

THE WALK

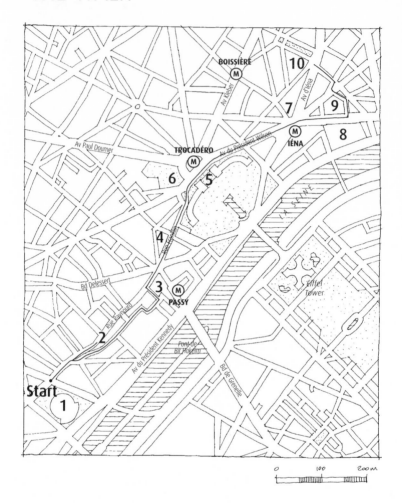

KEY

1. Musée de Radio-France
2. Maison de Balzac
3. Musée du Vin
4. Rue Franklin
5. Palais de Chaillot
6. Cimetière de Passy
7. Musée National des Arts Asiatiques Guimet
8. Palais de Tokyo
9. Musée Galliera
10. Musée du Cristal de Baccarat

Trocadéro

Musée de Radio-France ❶

Leave the Passy metro station and turn right onto Avenue du Président Kennedy. Musée de Radio-France will be on your right at No. 116. This museum traces the history of communications from the 18th century to the present day. It is housed in Maison de Radio-France, a massive circular office building that was built by Henri Bernard in 1963. The headquarters of the state-run radio station, this building houses more than 70 radio studios where programmes are made as well as an auditorium, which is open to the public. The building covers an area of 2 hectares (five acres) and is the single largest structure in the country.

Musée de Radio-France
Opening times: For tours only Mon–Sat
Closed public hols
Website: www.radiofrance.fr
Tel: 01. 56 40 15 16

Maison de Balzac ❷

From the Musée de Radio-France turn right onto rue Raynouard and Maison de Balzac will be on your right at No. 47. Writer Honoré de Balzac lived in this charming little house between 1840 and 1847. He stayed here under the assumed name of Monsieur de Brugnol in an effort to avoid his many creditors, and also wrote some of his most famous work here, including *La Cousine Bette* in 1846. The garden is perched on the steep hillside and affords wonderful views. The house contains drawings and paintings portraying Balzac, his family and close friends, as well as a reference library with some of his original work and a museum. There is a room dedicated to Madame Hanska, the Russian woman who corresponded with Balzac for almost 20 years and then married him in the final months of his life. He died in 1850.

Maison de Balzac
Opening times: 10am–6pm Tue–Sun (last admission 5pm)
Closed public hols
Website: www.balzac.paris.fr
Tel: 01. 55 74 41 80

Did You Know?
Maison de Balzac has a rear entrance leading onto the rue Berton, this is where the writer used to slip out of the house when he wanted to evade unwanted callers.

Musée du Vin ❸

Retrace your steps down rue Raynouard and take the very
sharp left onto rue Berton. This part of the city is almost like
an old country town, with its winding lanes and high stone
walls. It also provides unexpectedly delightful views of the Eiffel Tower. Follow
rue Berton as it winds between the stone walls and you will come to Avenue
Marcel Proust. Follow this as it veers to the right and then take the next left
onto rue Charles Dickens. The Musée du Vin will be in the far corner on your
left at the top of rue des Eaux.

This fascinating little museum is devoted to explaining wine-making.
Dioramas with waxwork figures and cardboard cut-outs illustrate how this
is done in the museum's atmospheric, vaulted cellars, which were once the
property of the monks of Passy. On show are collections of wine bottles, glasses
and corkscrews, as well as a selection of scientific instruments used in wine-
making and bottling processes. Tours include a wine-tasting session and it is
also possible to buy wine. The museum is also home to an excellent restaurant.

Musée du Vin
Opening times: 10am–6pm Tue–Sun
Closed 24 Dec–1 Jan
Website: www.museeduvinparis.com
Tel: 01. 45 25 63 26

Rue Franklin ❹

Take the Passage des Eaux, a narrow stepped street up to rue Raynouard and
turn right. Cross the junction onto rue Franklin and No. 25 bis will be on your
left. Concrete was invented by the Romans who used it extensively throughout
their empire. As a material it has wonderful strength in compression, but is
very weak in tension. This means that it could be used for structural elements
like walls but not for roofs, as they tended to collapse under their own weight.
In the 1850s a French engineer, François Coignet, had the brilliant idea of
reinforcing concrete by threading it with steel rods and meshes. This finally
gave the material some tensile strength. This process was further developed
by François Hennebique, who patented it in 1892. It was used mainly for
industrial buildings, but No. 25 bis rue Franklin was the first residential building
to make use of this revolutionary new material.

A multi-storey apartment building built by the architect Auguste Perret
in 1903–04, the building's reinforced-concrete frame is clearly expressed on
the façade, though disguised by strips of ceramic tiling. The non-load-bearing
panels are also decorated in tiles. To make up for the lack of a courtyard the
building is U-shaped, which allows for more windows. The novel use of glass
block for the staircase and bathrooms to the rear also enabled the architect
to build right to the edge of the property.

Trocadéro

Perret was the son of a builder and had trained, along with his younger brother Gustave, at the Ecole des Beaux Arts. He left without a diploma so that he could work for the family firm. Perret was following in the tradition of structural integrity championed by theorists such as Viollet-le-Duc, Choisy and Gaudet, and he thought that reinforced concrete was an ideal material to achieve this. Ironically, the concrete frame for this building was sub-contracted to another builder as the Perrets' firm felt that it would be too complicated for them at the time.

Palais de Chaillot ❺

Continue along rue Franklin and you will come to the Palais de Chaillot on your right overlooking Place du Trocadéro. The **Place du Trocadéro** was laid out as part of the Universal Exposition in 1878. Initially it had been called Place du Roi-de-Rome, in honour of Napoleon's son. Sitting at the apex of Chaillot hill, Napoleon had wanted to build a massive palace for his son, which would look out over the Seine and was well outside the city at the time. By his downfall the palace had barely started.

At the centre of Place du Trocadéro is a **statue of Marshal Foch**, France's military commander at the end of World War I. Built by Robert Wlérick and Raymond Martin, it commemorated the centenary of Foch's birth as well as the 22nd anniversary of the 1918 armistice and was unveiled on 11 November 1951. The **Palais de Chaillot** was built for the International Exposition, or World's Fair, that was held in Paris in 1937. Constructed between 1935 and 1937 it replaced an earlier building, the Palais du Trocadéro, which was built for the 1878 Universal Exposition. Designed by Jacques Carlu, Louis-Hippolyte Boileau and Léon Azéma, it houses exhibition and concert halls and terminates the grand axis that runs from the Ecole Militaire through the Champ-de-Mars and the Eiffel Tower.

The parvis or square between the two pavilions features large bronze sculptures and ornamental pools and is one of the most popular places in the city to take photographs of the Eiffel Tower. The terrace in front of the parvis contains two bronzes, *Apollo* by Henri Bouchard and *Hercules* by Albert Pommier and stairways lead down to the Théâtre National de Chaillot, which is well known for its avant-garde productions. The Palais itself consists of two massive curved wings, culminating in pavilions. It is chastely decorated with stylish Art Deco sculptures and bas-reliefs. The walls of the pavilions feature inscriptions in gold by the poet Paul Valéry.

The **Jardin du Trocadéro** covers 10 hectares (25 acres) and slope their way down to the Seine. They were designed by Lardat after the International Exposition of 1937 and consist of meandering walkways, clumps of trees and little streams crossed by pretty bridges. Sitting at the centre of the gardens is a long rectangular pool with fountains that operate in sequence. Massive water cannons fire jets of water in the direction of the Eiffel Tower. These were designed by Roger-Henri Expert, who was also responsible for the dramatic floodlighting. The pool is bordered by stone and gilt-bronze statues, including *Man* by Traverse, *Woman* by Braque, *Bull* by Jouve and *Horse* by Guyot.

Located in the east wing of the Palais de Chaillot is the **Cité de l'Architecture et du Patrimoine**. This shows the development of French architecture and includes gorgeous models of some of France's most famous cathedrals, including Chartres. The Galerie des Moulages covers the Middle Ages and Renaissance, while the Galerie Moderne et Contemporaine has a reconstruction of a Le Corbusier apartment. The museum also houses a school, a library and an archive, and is home to a number of heritage organisations.

The **Musée de l'Homme** is situated in the west wing of the palace and shows the history of human evolution from prehistory to the present day. Its anthropological exhibits come from all over the world. The **Musée de la Marine** traces France's maritime history and was set up by Charles X in 1827. It moved to this area in 1843 and contains some lovely scale-models of royal warships as well as navigational instruments and paintings. It also has a collection of memorabilia relating to the country's naval heroes.

Originally built for the 1878 Universal Exposition, **Cinéaqua** has been continuously modernised ever since and is now home to more than 500 species of fish and underwater life. The aquarium is located in what used to be a quarry and has been designed to merge into the hillside. Its entrance is at No. 5 Avenue Albert de Mun. The complex includes a cinema that combines film and aquarium technology, and there is also a Japanese restaurant whose main wall is part of the aquarium.

Cité de l'Architecture et du Patrimoine
Opening times: 11am–7pm Mon and Wed, 11am–9pm Fri–Sun
Website: www.citechaillot.fr
Tel: 01. 58 51 52 00

Sculpture, Jardins de Chaillot

Trocadéro

Musée de l'Homme
Opening times: 10am–5pm Mon and Wed–Fri, 10am–6pm Sat and Sun
Closed public hols
Website: www.mnhn.fr
Tel: 01. 44 05 72 72

Musée de la Marine
Opening times: 10am–6pm Wed–Mon
Closed 1 Jan, 1 May, 25 Dec
Website: www.musee-marine.fr
Tel: 01. 53 65 69 69

Cinéaqua
Opening times: 10am–8pm daily
Website: www.cineaqua.com
Tel: 01. 40 69 23 23

Cimetière de Passy ❻
Facing the Palais de Chaillot across Place du Trocadéro is the Cimetière de Passy. Its entrance is at No. 2 rue du Commandant-Shloesing. This small cemetery is not visited by tourists much but is an interesting place to wander in as there are more famous people buried here for its size than any other cemetery in Paris – probably because this has always been such a desirable place to live. It opened in 1820 and is the last resting place of composers Debussy and Fauré as well as the painter Manet, not to mention any number of politicians and public figures.

Cimetière de Passy
Opening times: 8am–6pm Mon–Fri, 8.30am–6pm Sat, 9am–6pm Sun
Tel: 01. 47 27 51 42

Musée National des Arts ❼
Asiatiques Guimet
Leave Place du Trocadéro via Avenue du Président Wilson and the Musée National des Arts Asiatiques Guimet will be on your left overlooking Place d'Iéna. This imposing museum, with its signature round tower overlooking the Place, contains one of the most important collections of Asian art anywhere in the world. It also has, thanks to France's former colonial ties to Southeast Asia, one of the finest collections of Khmer (or Cambodian) art in the West.

Originally established by industrialist Emile Guimet in Lyons in 1879, the collection moved to Paris in 1884 and represents every important artistic tradition in Asia, from India, through Southeast Asia, to China and Japan. It contains more than 45,000 works of art, including some particularly unusual

Palais de Tokyo

collections, such as sculptures from Angkor Wat and 1,600 Himalayan artworks. Other highlights include lacquer ware and bronzes from China, as well as a number of Buddhas. In fact, there is a **Panthéon Bouddhique** housed in additional gallery space located at No. 19 Avenue d'Iéna. Tea ceremonies are sometimes held here (enquire for details).

Musée National des Arts Asiatiques Guimet
Opening times: 10am–6pm Wed–Mon (last admission 5.30pm)
Website: www.museeguimet.fr
Tel: 01. 56 52 53 00

Panthéon Bouddhique
Opening times: 10am–6pm Wed–Mon (last admission 5.30pm)
Website: www.museeguimet.fr
Tel: 01. 40 73 88 00

Palais de Tokyo ❽

Continue along Avenue du Président-Wilson and the Palais de Tokyo will be on your right. Built for the 1937 International Exposition, it was originally called the Palais des Musées d'art moderne (Palace of the Museums of Modern

Trocadéro

Art). The Palais is a stark symmetrical Art Deco masterpiece overlooking the Seine and takes its name from Avenue de Tokio, which was changed to Avenue de New-York in 1945. Designed by architects Dondel, Aubert, Viard and Dastugue, it consists of two blocks linked by a colonnaded terrace looking out over the Seine. There is also an open-air café which has stunning views of the Eiffel Tower.

The building consists of two separate establishments dedicated to modern and contemporary art. The east wing belongs to the City of Paris and is home to the **Musée d'Art Modern de la Ville de Paris**. This is where the city's collection of modern art is displayed. Highlights include works by Modigliani, Rouault and Matisse (with two versions of *La Danse*), as well as Dufy's famous mural *La Fée Electricité*. The west wing of the Palais houses the **Site de création contemporaine** (Site of Contemporary Creation), which opened in 2002 and belongs to the state. The complex is also home to the **Pavillon**. Established in 2001, this is an experimental studio and laboratory space for resident artists and curators who are invited to work here.

Palais de Tokyo
Opening times: Noon–midnight Tue–Sun (to 10pm Wed)
Website www.palaisdetokyo.com
Tel: 01. 47 23 54 01

Musée d'Art Modern de la Ville de Paris
Opening times: 10am–6pm Tue–Sun (to 10pm Thur)
Website: www.mam.paris.fr
Tel: 01. 53 67 40 00

Musée Galliera

Musée Galliera ❾

Continue along Avenue du Président-Wilson and turn left onto rue de Galliera, then left onto Avenue Pierre I de Serbie and the Musée Galliera will be on your left. Also known as

the **Musée de la Mode de la Ville de Paris**, this museum is devoted to the evolution of fashion. It opened in 1977 in the Renaissance style palace built for the Duchess of Galliera in 1892. The collection comprises approximately 70,000 items, ranging from 18th-century clothing to underwear and accessories. It also includes clothes worn by famous women, including Marie-Antoinette, the Empress Josephine and Grace Kelly. It even includes the famous black dress worn by Audrey Hepburn in *Breakfast at Tiffany's*.

Musée Galliera
Open for exhibitions only: 10am–6pm Tue–Sun (from 2pm on some public hols)
Website: www.galliera.paris.fr
Tel: 01. 56 52 86 00

Musée du Cristal de Baccarat ❿

Walk up rue de Chaillot and turn left onto rue Freycinet and Places des Etats-Unis will be across Avenue d'Iéna. **Place des États-Unis** is home to a number of embassies, including some of the wealthier Middle-Eastern ones, as well as, of course, the one that gives the square its name: the United States of America. This tree-lined square is about 140 metres long and 30 metres wide and is a pleasantly shady spot, popular with office workers during lunchtime.

Trocadéro

The park at the square's centre is called Square Thomas Jefferson and was, until 1888, home to a bronze model of the Statue of Liberty. This was a fundraising ploy to try and help finance the real one in New York, which is a symbol of French-American friendship. Overlooking this leafy square at No. 11 sits the **Musée du Cristal de Baccarat**. This is where the Baccarat crystal company, founded in Lorraine in 1764, exhibits some of its 1,200 articles. Items include pieces that were made for some of Europe's royal households.

Musée du Cristal de Baccarat

Opening times: 10am–6.30pm Mon–Sat
Website: www.baccarat.fr
Tel: 01. 40 22 11 00

Did You Know?

Place des États-Unis originally had another name, Place de Bitche, which honoured a village in northeast France that had resisted the Prussian invasion of 1870. When American Ambassador Levi P. Morton established his country's embassy here he asked if the name could be changed because of its unfortunate similarity to the English word for a female dog.

Link to the Champs-Elysées walk:
Continue up Avenue d'Iéna.

Musée du Cristal de Baccarat

Champs-Elysées

Nearest Metro: Charles de Gaulle Étoile
Approximate walking time: 1 hour 30 minutes

Champs-Elysées

The Champs-Elysées is the most famous street in Paris, if not the world. Wide and tree-lined, it forms the main section of the grand axis that runs from the Louvre all the way to La Défense, a distance of 10 kilometres (6 miles). With its numerous shops, cafés and restaurants, the area is one of the best places to shop in the city, as it is home to Avenue Montaigne as well as the rue du Faubourg St-Honoré. The focal point of the area is the Arc de Triomphe, the massive triumphal arch built at the western end of the Champs-Elysées to celebrate Napoleon's victories. At the eastern end of the avenue is a cluster of grand buildings, the Grand Palais and the Petit Palais, which nestle amidst the lovely Jardins des Champs-Elysées and overlook the beautiful Pont Alexandre III, one of the most beautiful bridges in the city. This is also home to the Palais de l'Elysée, the official residence of the President of France.

THE WALK

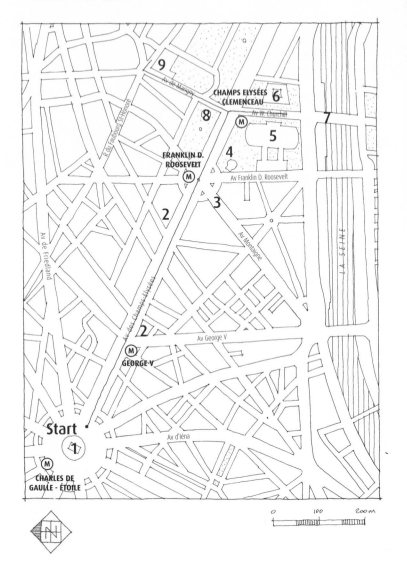

9

CHAMPS ELYSÉES
- CLEMENCEAU 6

Av de Matigny

Av W. Churchill

7

M

8

5

FRANKLIN D.
ROOSEVELT 4

M

Av Franklin D. Roosevelt

R. du Faubourg St-Honoré

3

2

Av Montaigne

Av de Friedland

Av de Champs-Élysées

LA SEINE

2

Av George V

M

GEORGE V

Start

Av d'Iéna

1

M

CHARLES DE
GAULLE - ÉTOILE

0   100   200m

KEY

1. Arc de Triomphe
2. Avenue des Champs-Elysées
3. Avenue Montaigne
4. Jardins des Champs-Elysées
5. Grand Palais
6. Petit Palais
7. Pont Alexandre III
8. Théâtre Marigny
9. Palais de l'Elysée

Arc de Triomphe

Arc de Triomphe ❶

Exit Charles de Gaulle Étoile metro station and you will be at the Arc de Triomphe. After the Battle of Austerlitz, Napoleon's most celebrated victory in 1805, he promised his men that 'You shall go home beneath triumphal arches'. The first stone of this monumental Arc de Triomphe was laid the following year. Designed by architect Jean Chalgrin, it is a simple arch with a vaulted passageway topped by an attic. Its four pillars feature allegorical sculptural reliefs. The simplicity of its form is deceptive, for this is a massive building, standing 50 metres (164 feet) tall. Delays in construction and Napoleon's fall from power meant that the arch wasn't completed until 1836. It forms the focal point of Place Charles de Gaulle Etoile, another of Haussmann's urban interventions. Twelve avenues radiate in different directions to from a vast star. Some of these commemorate military leaders such as Foch, Marceau and MacMahon.

Simply known as Place de l'Étoile until Charles de Gaulle's death in 1969, it was renamed in his honour – the old name seems to have stuck, however. The arch is the starting point for France's most important celebrations and parades and its viewing platform commands one of the best views in the city.

The arch sports some magnificent sculptural reliefs, including Jean-Pierre Cortot's *The Triumph of Napoleon* from 1810. This depicts Napoleon wearing a toga and being crowned with a laurel wreath to commemorate the Treaty of Vienna, signed that same year. *The Departure of the Volunteers of '92* is by François Rude and is also known as *La Marseillaise*. It shows figures being led by Bellona, the goddess of war, who seem to have been so excited by their patriotic fervour that they have forgotten to put on any clothes. Two reliefs by Antoine Etex show *Resistance*, which features an equestrian figure and a naked soldier protecting his family under the watchful eye of the spirit of the future, and *Peace*, where a warrior is seen sheathing his sword surrounded by the accoutrements of agriculture under the benign gaze of Minerva, the goddess of wisdom.

The attic is decorated by 30 shields, while the arch's inner walls bear the name of 558 French generals – those who died in battle have their names underlined. The names of the 128 battles fought by the Republican and Napoleonic regimes are also carved into the vault. The Tomb of the Unknown Soldier (from World War I) stands in front of the arch, with an eternal flame that faces down the avenue.

Arc de Triomphe
Opening times: 10am–11pm daily, Apr–Sept; 10am–10.30pm daily, Oct–Mar (last admission 30 mins earlier)
Closed 1 Jan, 1 May, 8 May, 14 Jul, 11 Nov, 25 Dec
Website: www.monum.fr
Tel: 01. 55 37 73 77

Avenue des Champs-Elysées ❷

Walk down the Avenue des Champs-Elysées. This famous thoroughfare began as a tree-lined avenue leading to the Palais des Tuileries. Laid out by royal gardener André Le Nôtre in 1667, it was intended to extend the view from the royal palace. It eventually became known as the Champs-Elysées, taking is name from the Elysian Fields (heaven) of Greek mythology. Planned as a triumphal way, it complements the massive Arc de Triomphe and is the route of France's national parades, including the annual Bastille Day celebration.

In the second half of the 19th century, the Avenue became extremely fashionable and its most famous cafés and restaurants date from that period. **Le Fouquet's**, which occupies the strategic corner of the Champs-Elysées and Avenue Georges V, was recently renovated by Jacques Garcia. This restaurant has been an icon since it opened in 1899. A traditional brasserie, it is also a café with a large terrace overlooking the avenue. Invariably packed, it is a pleasant place to sit and watch the world go by, despite the expense.

Walking down the Champs-Elysées you will notice that it is not quite as

Citroen building, Avenue des Champs-Elysées

upmarket as it once was. Cinemas, generic chain-stores and fast-food outlets have taken over from the chic boutiques of the early 20th century, but it is still an impressive street to stroll along. It is also home to some interesting architecture, including the recently built **Citroën** showroom at No. 42 (on the left after the junction with the rue du Colisée). André Citroën first displayed his Type A car at this prestigious showroom in 1919 and the company decided to renovate the premises in 2004 (it had been occupied by a restaurant chain for several years). They chose architect Manuelle Gautrand, whose design has made full use of the building's narrow site to create an eye-catching 25-metre-high sculptural façade. This is formed of seven superimposed rotating platforms, the glazing of which has been cleverly designed to form the Citroën logo.

Le Fouquet's
Website: www.fouquets-barriere.com
Tel: 01. 40 69 60 50

Citroën
Website: www.citroen.com

Avenue Montaigne ❸

Continue along the Champs-Elysées and you will come to the Rond Point des Champs-Elysées. Avenue Montaigne will be on your right. This street is named in honour of the French Renaissance writer Michel de Montaigne, but was originally known as the Allée des Veuves (Widows' Avenue), because of the recently-bereaved women who used to gather here to comfort one another.

Now the world's most expensive shopping street, it is home to some of the most celebrated names in fashion, including Christian Dior at No. 30, Valentino at Nos. 17–19 and Chanel at No. 42. The celebrated jewellers Henry Winston and Bulgari are at Nos. 29 and 45 respectively, while the Plaza Athenée Hotel is the preferred stopping-off point for the international elite who frequent these temples of taste. In the 19th century Avenue Montaigne was famous for its dance halls and a Winter Garden.

Did You Know?
It was in the Avenue Montaigne's Winter Garden that people first heard a new instrument being played by its inventor, Adolphe Sax, which he named the saxophone.

Jardins des Champs-Elysées ❹

Continue along the Champs-Elysées and you will see the Jardins des Champs-Elysées on either side of the avenue. These charming gardens, with their

Champs-Elysées

formal layouts of flowerbeds, paths, fountains and pavilions, have hardly changed since they were created by architect Jacques Hittorff in 1838. Their heyday was at the end of the 19th and early 20th centuries, when fashionable Parisians would promenade here, including a young Marcel Proust. The gardens were the location for a World Fair held in Paris in 1855, when the Palais de l'Industrie was built. This was replaced by the Grand Palais and the Petit Palais, both of which were built for the Universal Exposition of 1900.

Grand Palais ❺

Located on the Avenue Franklin D. Roosevelt side of the Jardins des Champs-Elysées is the **Théâtre du Rond-Point**. This small theatre was home to the Renaud-Barrault Company. Established in 1860, it was originally called the Panorama National and later became known as the Palais des Glaces, which was of the Paris' most popular attractions around 1900. It only became a proper theatre in 1981, when the company that had been using the old Gare d'Orsay were obliged to leave the former railway station to allow it to be converted into a museum.

Completely remodelled and redecorated in 1995, the theatre specialises in modern plays, usually by living playwrights. It also has a small, stylish restaurant that serves an excellent afternoon tea. The plaques on the theatre's rear door feature Napoleon's military campaigns.

Sitting just behind the Théâtre du Rond-Point is the vast bulk of the **Grand Palais**, its entrance is via Porte A on Avenue Général Eisenhower. Built along with the Petit Palais and the Gare (now Musée) d'Orsay for the Universal Exposition of 1900, this imposing glass-roofed exhibition hall has recently been restored. Intended as a monument to the glory of French art, it is still home to major international exhibitions today. Temporary exhibitions are held in the Galerie Nationales du Grand Palais. The Palais also contains a pleasant restaurant. The Palais was designed by Deglane, Louvet and Thomas, and its massive structure combines an imposing Beaux Arts stone façade with beautiful Art Nouveau ironwork. Covering 15,000 square metres (160,000 square feet), the building's chief glory is the glass-and-iron roof, which is capped by a vast dome. The corners overlooking Avenue Winston Churchill are graced by two dramatic Récipon sculptures: *L'Harmonie Triomphant de la Discorde* (near the Seine) and *L'Immortalité Devançant le Temps* (at the Champs-Elysées). Each features a triumphant human figure guiding four horses skyward. The Palais' façade is also decorated by a 75-metre-long (246 feet) mosaic, *Les Grandes Epoques de l'Art* by Louis Edouard Fournier.

The **Palais de la Découverte** is part of the Grand Palais and its entrance is on Avenue Franklin D. Roosevelt. This opened as a separate wing of the Grand Palais at the time of the Universal Exposition in 1937. It is a popular science museum and includes a planetarium.

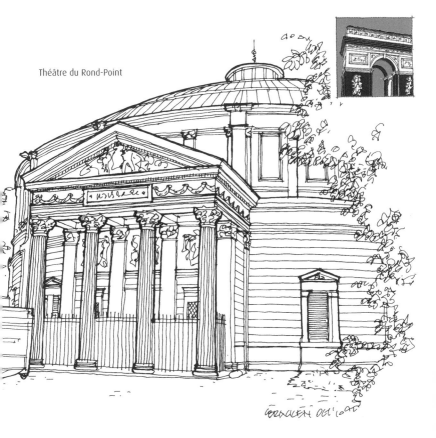

Théâtre du Rond-Point

Théâtre du Rond-Point
Website: www.theatredurondpoint.fr
Tel : 01. 44 95 98 00

Grand Palais
Opening times: For temporary exhibitions (usually 10am–8pm Thur–Mon, 10am–10pm Wed, but call to check)
Closed 1 May, 25 Dec
Website: www.grandpalais.fr
Tel: 01. 44 13 17 17

Palais de la Découverte
Opening times: 9.30am–6pm Tue–Sat, 10am–7pm Sun
Closed 1 Jan, 1 May, 14 Jul, 15 Aug, 25 Dec
Website: www.plais-decouverte.fr
Tel: 01. 56 43 20 21

> **Did You Know?**
> The metal structure supporting the glass roof of the Grand Palais weighs 8,500 tonnes; 1,500 more than the Eiffel Tower.

Champs-Elysées

Petit Palais ❻

Sitting opposite the Grand Palais on Avenue Winston Churchill is the Petit Palais. This gem of a building was built, like the Grand Palais opposite, for the Universal Exposition of 1900. It was intended to house a major display of French art and is now home to the Musée des Beaux-arts de la Ville de Paris (the City of Paris Beaux Arts Museum). The building's trapezoidal plan encloses a semi-circular garden courtyard surrounded by a colonnade. Designed by Charles Girault, with distinct echoes of Garnier, it is entirely lit by natural light. Similar in style to the Grand Palais, its Ionic columns, grand porch and dome also echo Les Invalides across Pont Alexandre III.

The Cours de la Reine, which is nearest the river, is used for temporary exhibitions, while the Champs-Elysées side is home to the Palais' permanent collections, which are divided into different sections: Greek, Roman, medieval and Renaissance ivories and sculptures; Renaissance clocks and jewellery; and 17th-, 18th- and 19th-century art and furniture. The Palais also exhibits a number of Impressionist artworks.

Petit Palais
Opening times: 10am–6pm Tue–Sun
Closed public hols
Website: www.petitpalais-paris.fr
Tel: 01. 53 43 40 00

Pont Alexandre III

Pont Alexandre III ❼

At the end of Avenue Winston Churchill sits the Pont Alexandre III. Generally regarded as the prettiest bridge in Paris, it was named in honour of Tsar Alexander III of Russia, who laid the foundation stone in 1896. It was seen as a concrete sign of the alliance the two countries had just made. After France's disastrous defeat at the hands of the Prussians in 1871, she wanted to prevent any such attack from happening again and so forged this alliance with Russia to ensure that the next time the Germans tried to invade they would be forced to fight on two fronts (which is indeed what happened in World War I, and the main reason why Germany lost). The two countries made an unlikely pair: France was the bastion of democracy, while Russia was the last absolute monarchy in Europe – they were known as Beauty and the Beast.

The bridge was completed in time for the Universal Exposition in 1900, and its style indeed reflects the Grand Palais and Petit Palais that overlook it. Full of exuberant Beaux Art decoration, with lamps, nymphs (by Georges Récipon) and lions (by Jules Dalou), the bridge is actually a masterpiece of 19th-century engineering. It forms a single span 6 metres (18 feet) high across the Seine, this was done to prevent the bridge from obscuring the views of Les Invalides or the Champs-Elysées. The massive pylons at either end help to anchor the piers and absorb the immense forces generated by such a large span.

Théâtre Marigny

Retrace your steps back to the Avenue des Champs-Elysées and walk up Avenue de Marigny. The Théâtre Marigny will be on your left. This site has been used as a showplace by travelling showmen since at least 1835. After the revolution of 1848 a small theatre, the Château d'Enfer, was set up here. It was also known as the Salle Lacaze after its founder, and presented a variety of shows.

When the Salle Lacaze was forced to close down, Jacques Offenbach (composer of the famous *Cancan*) opened the Théâtre des Bouffes-Parisiens in 1855. It benefitted from some of the overspill from the Universal Exposition that year. It was soon renamed the theatre Bouffes d'Été, since Offenbach was director of the 'Bouffes d'Hiver' in the Salle Choiseul on rue Monsigny. Offenbach premiered a number of his pieces here but the lease ran out in 1858 and it became the Théâtre Debureau. It was taken over two more times before being demolished in 1881 to make way for the current building, which was built by Charles Garnier in 1883 as a Panorama, which explains its unusual twelve-sided shape. Converted into a theatre once more in 1894, it was enlarged and modernised in 1925.

Throughout the 1930s the Théâtre Marigny was a popular venue for musical theatre, which even included some Offenbach revivals. Today it is noted for its modern French drama.

Palais de l'Elysée ❾

Continue up Avenue de Marigny and turn right. The Palais de l'Elysée will be on the corner on your right at No. 55 rue du Faubourg St-Honoré. This has been the official residence of the President of the Republic since 1874. It was originally called the Hôtel d'Evreux after the man who built it in 1718, the Compte d'Evreux.

The building is a beautiful example of 18th-century French Neoclassicism, while its interior contains a series of different decorative styles, reflecting the different people who have lived in it. Napoleon's sister Caroline lived here with her husband from 1805 to 1808 and two lovely rooms have been preserved from this period: the Salon Murat (after Caroline's husband) and the Salon d'Argent. There is also a *salle de bains* (bathroom) built for the Empress Eugénie which was designed by architect Eugène Lacroix in the 1850s. General de Gaulle used to hold press conferences in the Hall of Mirrors, while the Presidential apartments on the first floor are now decorated in a more convenient modern style.

Napoleon III plotted the coup that turned him from France's first president into its last emperor here, while some other famous residents have included Louis XV's mistress Madame de Pompadour, Napoleon himself, and Tsar Alexander III of Russia. The rear of the palace looks out onto a beautiful English garden.

Champs-Elysées

Did You Know?
The Elysée Palace is where Napoleon signed his abdication after the defeat at Waterloo in 1815.

Link to the Opéra walk: Continue along the rue du Faubourg St-Honoré and turn left at rue Royale.

Opéra

Nearest Metro: Madeleine
Approximate walking time: 1 hour 30 minutes

Opéra

The Opéra district is where Baron Haussmann built his grandest boulevards, as well as the magnificent opera house which gives the area its name. In addition to this sumptuous Second Empire edifice are the imposing Madeleine, the Palais de la Bourse and the original Bibliothèque Nationale.

The boulevards in this part of Paris are home to some of the city's best shopping, with a number of top department stores, including Au Printemps and Galeries Lafayette, as well as the quainter *passages*, the covered arcades that were the prototype for the shopping centre.

Two of Paris' most celebrated food shops are also located here, Fauchon and Hédiard, as well as some entertaining museums: the Paris Story covers the history of the city, while the Musée Grévin features delightful 19th-century waxworks.

THE WALK

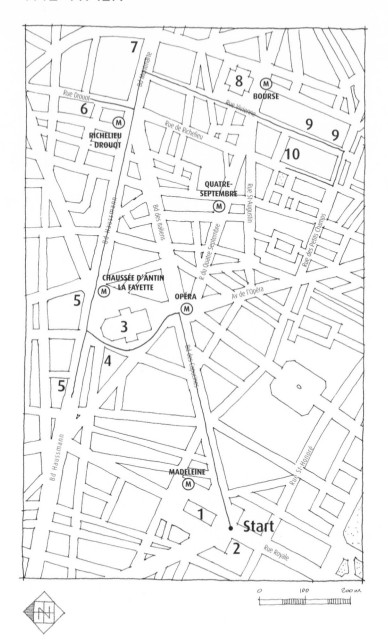

KEY

Opéra

La Madeleine

La Madeleine ❶

Exit the Madeleine metro station and you will be at La Madeleine. Commissioned by Napoleon as a temple to the glory of his Grande Armée, this magnificent essay in regal Neoclassicism was designed by Pierre-Alexandre Vignon, an Inspector-General of Buildings.

This imposing location, sitting at the top of the axis that runs across the Place de la Concorde from the Assemblée Nationale Palais-Bourbon, is a fitting spot for this peristyle temple which contains 52 20-metre-high (66-foot) fluted Corinthian columns. It is approached by grand flights of steps at either end. The pediment sculpture is by Philippe-Henri Lemaire and shows Mary Magdalene at the Last Judgement, while the bas-reliefs on the great bronze doors show the Ten Commandments by Henri de Triqueti. The interior makes lavish use of gilt and marble and contains some fine sculpture, particularly François Rude's *Baptism of Christ*. The church was reconsecrated to St Mary Magdalene by Louis XVIII in 1842. Place de la Madeleine was created to set off this magnificent church and is a mecca for gourmets.

Fauchon at No. 26 is nicknamed the 'millionaires' supermarket' and sells more than 20,000 different items. **Hediard** at No. 21 is noted for its wines, cheeses and chocolate. They also blend their own tea, which is shipped all over the world. The large house at No. 9 is where Marcel Proust grew up, while to the east of the church there is a small but busy flower market.

La Madeleine
Opening times: 7am–7pm daily
Tel: 01. 44 51 69 00

Fauchon
Website: www.fauchon.com
Tel: 01. 70 39 38 00

Hediard
Website: www.hediard.com
Tel: 01. 43 12 88 88

Flower Market
Opening times: 8am–7.30pm Tue–Sun

Village Royal ❷

Between rue Royale and rue Boissy d'Anglas sits a charming little cité – a type of self-enclosed residential enclave typical of Paris. Formerly the home of glass-workers and silversmiths, it nestles amidst a distinctly fashionable part of the city and contained a number of excellent 18th-century town houses, including the former home of the Duchesse d'Abrantès.

The cité was converted into an open-air shopping mall in 1994 by the architect Laurent Bourgois, who has married its classic charm with convenient modern elements to create an extremely stylish place to shop in. It can be approached from both sides, with the rue Royale entrance located at No. 25. It is now home to a number of upmarket shops, including Chanel and Dior. There is also a lovely café.

Village Royal
Opening times: 8am–8.30pm Mon–Sat
Shops: 10am–7pm
Website: www.villageroyal.com

Shop, rue du Faubourg St-Honoré

Opéra National de ❸ Paris Garnier

Walk up Boulevard de la Madeleine, which turns into Boulevard des Capucines, and you will pass the Café de la Paix on your left. This famous Parisian institution still has its 19th-century interior, which was designed by Charles Garnier. Continue along Boulevard des Capucines and the Opéra National de Paris Garnier will be on your left, centred majestically on the **Avenue de l'Opéra**, which is one of the most famous of the broad boulevards built by Baron Haussmann in the 1860s and '70s. Much of the medieval city (including a mound from which Joan of Arc began her crusade against the English invaders) was razed to make way for these bold new avenues.

The Avenue de l'Opéra, which runs north from the side of the Louvre to the Opéra, was completed in 1876. One of the striking features of the boulevards is their uniformity. Lined with five-storey sandstone apartment buildings, with shops on the ground floor, they are decorated with stone carvings, wrought-iron railings and mansard roofs. Lined with plane trees, these rigorously rigid avenues are in stark contrast to some of the streets that cross them, often at odd angles, which reflects the older medieval fabric from which they were so brutally cut in the 19th century.

The **Opéra National de Paris Garnier** was conceived as a centrepiece of the boulevards. This Second Empire opera house is a flamboyant neo-Baroque confection. Designed by Charles Garnier, construction started in 1862 and wasn't completed until 1875, having been interrupted by the Franco-Prussian War and the 1871 Commune that followed it. The building's functions can clearly be identified by the different parts of the external structure, for example, the cupola above the auditorium sits in front of the triangular pediment that rises over the stage. The façade is actually very well proportioned, but its Neoclassical rigour is somewhat disguised by an over-exuberant decoration. This makes generous use of stone, marble and bronze to form a mix of styles all topped off by numerous statues, including the gilt Apollo, Poetry and Music by Aimé Millet at the apex of the opera house's green copper roof. Garnier personally supervised the building's decorative scheme and commissioned 73 painters and 14 sculptors to work on it.

The interior consists of a traditional Italian-style auditorium arranged in five tiers with 2,200 seats. Awash with red velvet, chubby cherubs and gold leaf, it also has a ceiling that was painted by Marc Chagall in 1964. The stage can accommodate 450 performers. Garnier saw the opera as a ceremony celebrating man's primitive instincts in a ritual coming together of shared dreams, so the spectators were there not only to see but also be seen. The evening's drama started the moment they entered the foyer, which is why Garnier provided such a generously sweeping marble-and-onyx staircase and so many mirrors. In fact, the foyers and staircases take up more space than the theatre itself. Although no longer used as an opera house – that function has been taken over by the Opéra National de Paris Bastille – ballet is still performed here.

The **Musée de l'Opéra** is located in what used to be Napoleon III's private entrance to the opera house. An attempt had been made on the Emperor's life in 1858, and as this had occurred outside the old opera house, Garnier provided a pavilion with curved ramps so that the Emperor could safely step from his carriage into the suite of rooms that led to the royal box. The museum highlights the history of opera via its collection of musical scores and manuscripts, as well as photographs and artists' memorabilia. There are also models of stage sets and busts of famous composers. The museum is also home to an excellent library of books and manuscripts on theatre, dance and music.

Did You Know?

Underneath the Opéra National de Paris Garnier is a small lake which provided the inspiration for Paul Leroux's *Phantom of the Opera.*

Opéra National de Paris Garnier
Opening times: 10am–5pm daily (1pm on show days)
Website: www.operadeparis.fr
Tel: 08. 92 89 90 90

Musée de l'Opéra
Opening times: 10am–5pm daily
Closed 1 Jan, 1 May
Tel: 08. 92 89 90 90

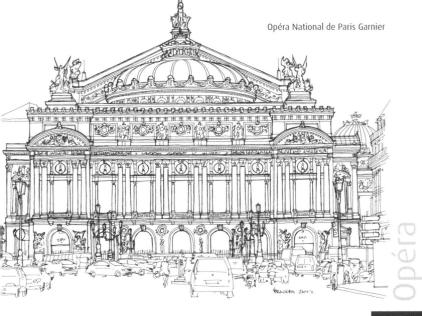

Opéra National de Paris Garnier

opéra

Paris Story ❹

Located across rue Scribe from the Opéra is the Paris Story museum at No. 11 bis. This museum is very useful for anyone visiting Paris for the first time. It explains the history and geology of the city in an hour-long film and interactive display. This covers the 2,000 years of history from the Gallo-Roman settlement of Lutèce right up to the present day. The show is narrated by a holograph of the writer Victor Hugo. There is also a 3D model of the city, which allows visitors to point to various monuments and get to know their history. The Explore Paris gallery consists of five TV screens showing 3D films of the city.

Paris Story
Opening times: 10am–6pm daily
Website: www.paris-story.com
Tel: 01. 42 66 62 06

Les Grands Boulevards ❺ 🎫 📷 🎁 📮 🎮 🛍

Continue up rue Scribe and you will come to Boulevard Haussmann. This is home to some of the most famous department stores in Paris, including Au Printemps and Galeries Lafayette. The word boulevard comes from the old Dutch word *bulwerc*, which means bulwark or rampart. These eight grands boulevards – Madeleine, Capucines, Italiens, Montmartre, Poissonnière, Bonne Nouvelle, St-Denis and St-Martin – describe a great arc that runs from La Madeleine to Place de la Republique and were originally the city's fortifications.

They were rendered obsolete in the 17th century and became famous in the 19th when the fashionable citizens of Paris used to promenade up and down them in their finery. The word *boulevardier* was invented at this time to describe anyone who cut a dash on them. There is also the figure of the *flâneur*, a word coined by the poet Charles Baudelaire to describe a person who strolls aimlessly around the city. Most of the boulevards have become quite tatty now, their once-fine facades hidden behind vast advertising hoardings, but they are still popular, particularly with tourists and shoppers.

Boulevard Haussmann is famous for its huge department stores. **Galerie Lafayette** is located at No. 40 and is perhaps the city's most illustrious. This ten-story complex, opened by Theophile Bader and Alphonse Kahn in 1893, was originally a small department store on the corner of rue Lafayette and the rue de la Chaussee d'Antin. It increased substantially in size between 1896 and 1905 and then in 1912 they asked the architect Cahnautin to build its trademark stained-glass dome. Selling everything you might expect from a department store, it also has an excellent food hall, Lafayette Gourmet. One can enjoy breathtaking views of the city from the roof.

Au Printemps is located at No. 64 Boulevard Haussmann and is best known for its household goods and large menswear department. Printemps means 'spring' in French, and this is the flagship store of an international chain, with branches throughout France, the Middle and Far East. The business was rescued from collapse by a man called Gustave Laguionie in 1900 who then got architect René Binet to extend the premises along the Boulevard Haussmann in the Art Nouveau style. The building later burnt down, however, and its interior was rebuilt in the 1920s. One of its most striking features is the elaborate cupola above the main restaurant. This was dismantled and moved to Clichy in 1939 to avoid being damaged in World War II. It was restored in 1973 by the grandson of the original designer, using plans that had been kept in the family's archives.

Did You Know?
No. 14 Boulevard des Capucines is where the world's first film was shown, by the Lumière brothers in 1895. This momentous occasion took place in the Salon Indien of the Grand Café. There is a plaque commemorating the event.

Drouot ⑥

With the department stores on your left, continue along Boulevard Haussmann until you come to rue Drouot and turn left. The Hôtel des Ventes will be at No. 9 on the left. There has been an auction house here since 1858. Emperor Napoleon III is even said to have come here in 1860 to buy some earthenware pots. Named after the Compte de Drouot, an aide-de-camp to Napoleon, this is France's leading auction house (*hôtel des ventes*). It changed its name to Nouveau Drouot in the 1970s, when the old building was demolished and replaced by this rather unspectacular new one. The presence of such a famous auction house in the area has encouraged a number of antique shops to open nearby. There is an amazing view of Sacré-Coeur from this street, it seems to float above the city.

Drouot (Hôtel des Ventes)
Opening times: 11am–6pm Mon–Sat, sales 2pm
Website: www.drouot.fr
Tel: 01. 48 00 20 20

Musée Grévin ⑦

Retrace your steps down rue Drouot and turn left onto Boulevard Montmartre. The Musée Grévin will be on your left at No. 10. This delightful waxworks museum was founded in 1882 and is a remarkable place, especially for children. Famous figures are on show and there are a number of historical tableaux, including Louis XIV at home in Versailles and the arrest of Louis XVI. There is also a Cabinet Fantastique which contains funhouse mirrors and hosts regular magic shows. The star of the show has to be Le Palais des Mirages, a magical room that can transform itself from a topical jungle to a Hindu temple or a Moorish palace. This is done thanks to a cunning system of mirrors and props and dates from the 1900 Universal Exposition. Designed by the architect Emile Hénard, it was bought by Grevin after the Expo and installed in the museum.

Musée Grévin
Opening times: 10am–6.30pm Mon–Fri, 10am–7pm Sat and Sun (last admission 1 hour before closing)
Website: www.grevin.fr
Tel: 01. 47 70 85 05

Palais de la Bourse ❽

Retrace your steps up Boulevard Montmartre and turn left onto rue Vivienne. The Palais de la Bourse will be on your left after a short distance. The French stock exchange was founded by Napoleon to unify the various stock-trading activities that were taking place across the city. Housed between 1826 and 1987 in this imposing temple-like structure designed by architect Alexandre-Theodore Brongniart, it is a strict peristyle with a colonnade of Corinthian columns in light beige sandstone. Today the stock market has moved to No. 29 rue Cambon and this once busy Palais de la Bourse is used for the Matif (futures market) and the Monep (the traded options market).

Palais de la Bourse
Visits by appointment only
Tel: 01. 49 27 55 54

Palais de la Bourse

Les Passage ❾

Continue along rue Vivienne and you will come to one of the entrances to Galerie Vivienne, on your left at No. 6. This is one of a number of early 19th-century shopping arcades (also known as *passages* or *galeries*) which are located between the Boulevard Montmartre and the rue St-Marc. They were a brilliant innovation when first constructed as they allowed shoppers to browse in an environment free of traffic and protected from the elements. They were basically the precursor to the modern-day shopping centre.

These *passages* were a mecca not only for shoppers but also architects from all over Europe who came to marvel at their ingenuity, including Mengoni, who went on to build the Gallery Victor-Emmanuel II in Milan. Improvements made to the city by Baron Haussmann, such as pavements and sewers, meant that the *passages* lost some of their appeal from the 1860s onwards and fell into disuse. Some were revitalised in the 1970s and are home to an eclectic mix of shops. One of the most charming of them is the **Galerie Vivienne** (entrances at No. 6 rue Vivienne, No. 5 rue de la Banque and No. 4 rue des Petits Champs). It was constructed in 1826 from a design by Delannoy and contains mosaic floors (by Italian artist Faccina), iron-and-glass roofs, some interesting shops and an excellent tearoom.

The success of Galerie Vivienne led its developers to purchase the neighbouring 17th-century *hôtel particulier* which they demolished to make a second arcade. The **Galerie Colbert** never achieved the success of

Galerie Vivienne

its prestigious neighbour, even though it certainly has the same elegance, including a lovely glass-roofed rotunda. It was restored in 1986.

Galerie Vivienne
www.galerie-vivienne.com

Bibliothèque Nationale ❿

Wander Les Passages at will and exit onto rue des Petit Champs and turn right. Then take the next right onto rue de Richelieu and the Bibliothèque Nationale will be at No. 58 overlooking the small Square Louvois. The Bibliothèque Nationale (National Library) stems from the royal library established by King Charles V in the Louvre in the 14th century. This was then opened to the public by Louis XIV in 1692. Its collection was vastly increased during the Revolution by the addition of libraries confiscated from aristocrats and the clergy and it was made a national amenity in 1792.

Until recently it was housed in this beautiful but too-small town house. President Mitterrand commissioned a grand new library complex from architect Dominique Perrault in 1989 (see page 217). This is located behind the Gare d'Austerlitz. The library's collection, which includes two Gutenberg bibles, is housed in the new building, but a part of it is still housed here, including manuscripts by Victor Hugo and Marcel Proust. A law passed in 1537 means that every book printed in France has to have a copy here, but the library also has a superb collection of engravings and photographs, one of the best in the world in fact. It also has departments for maps, plans and musical scores.

This delightful building is the former palace of Cardinal Mazarin and contains some interiors by Mansart, which date from the 1640s. The library was established here in 1721, and its chief glory is the reading room by Henri Labrouste, which was built in 1868. Labrouste, who also designed the Sainte-Geneviève Library, created an airy, naturally-lit space with 16 slender metal columns crowned by foliage capitals. These support a cluster of nine domes made of glass and porcelain. This breathtakingly elegant space is surrounded by an arcade decorated in the Pompeian style and containing lunettes painted with scenes of the Jardins du Luxembourg.

Bibliothèque Nationale
Opening times: 9am–6pm Mon–Fri, 9am–5pm Sat
Website: www.bnf.fr
Tel: 01. 53 79 59 59

Link to the Montmartre walk: It is best get to Montmartre by metro. The nearest station to the Bibliothèque Nationale is Bourse. Walk to the top of rue de Richelieu and turn right onto rue St-Augustin, the station will be ahead of you.

Montmartre

Nearest Metro: Anvers
Approximate walking time: 2 hours

Montmartre

Walking around Montmartre (Martyrs' Mount) is like stepping back into the 19th century. This steep *butte*, or hill, has long been a haunt of Bohemian life but is now more a mecca for tourists. Artists, writers, poets and prostitutes crammed into the cosy bars and cafés, making this one of the city's liveliest, if louche, areas in the 19th century. The artistic world has long since vanished, but the streets are still charming, with their twisting cobbled lengths suddenly giving way to steep staircases leading down to tiny squares full of charm and character. There are even some surprising remnants of the area's rural past, with Paris' last vineyard and a number of windmills – including of course the world-famous Moulin-Rouge.

Place du Tertre is Montmartre's old village square and it is full of art stalls. For those with a more discerning eye, there is the Espace Dali Montmartre or La Halle Saint Pierre. Montmartre also has some wonderful architecture, including some interesting churches like St-Pierre de Montmartre and St-Jean l'Evangéliste de Montmartre, as well as the one that takes its name from the Christian martyrs that gave the area its name in the 3rd century: the Chapelle du Martyre. Of course no trip to Montmartre would be complete without a visit to the most spectacular church of them all, Sacré-Coeur – its front steps command simply unforgettable views of the city.

THE WALK

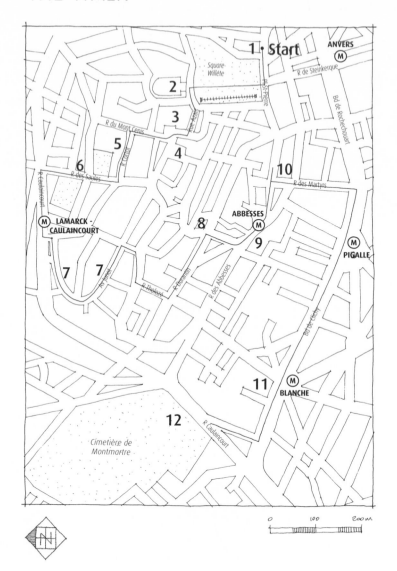

KEY

1. La Halle Saint Pierre
2. Sacré-Coeur
3. St-Pierre de Montmartre
4. Place du Tertre
5. Musée de Montmartre
6. Le Lapin Agile
7. Avenue Junot
8. Bateau-Lavoir
9. St-Jean l'Evangéliste de Montmartre
10. Chapelle du Martyre
11. Moulin Rouge
12. Cimetière de Montmartre

Montmartre

La Halle Saint Pierre ❶

Leave Anvers metro station and walk up rue de Steinkerque. Turn right onto Place St-Pierre and La Halle Saint Pierre will be on your left (entrance at No. 2 rue Ronsard). This unusual gallery, established by the French artist Jean Dubuffet in an old market building in 1945, exhibits what it known as Art Brut (outsider or marginal art, literally 'strong art'). This is work that has been created outside of society's usually culture, often by the patients at asylums or the mentally handicapped. It also exhibits some of the naïve art (self-taught artists' work) that was collected by the publisher Max Fourny. Home to an avant-garde theatre which stages musicals, it also hosts regular literary evenings, debates and children's workshops. There is also a bookshop and café.

La Halle Saint Pierre
Opening times: 10am–6pm daily
Website: www.hallesaintpierre.org
Tel: 01. 42 58 72 89

Sacré-Coeur ❷

To get to Sacré-Coeur from La Halle Saint Pierre you can either walk up the paths that wind their way through Square Willette, or take the funicular, a cable railway that runs from the bottom of the steeply sloping rue Foyatier. Metro tickets are valid. At the start of the Franco-Prussian War in 1870, two Roman Catholic businessmen, Alexandre Legentil and Hubert Rohault de Fleury, made a vow to build a church dedicated to the Sacred Heart of Jesus if the city was spared the Prussian invasion. Despite a humiliating defeat for the French, and a lengthy siege followed by the bloody Paris Commune, the city did indeed survive relatively unscathed.

Work began on the basilica in 1875 to a design by the architect Paul Abadie. Inspired by the Romano-Byzantine church of St-Front in Périgueux, it was completed in 1914, but World War I delayed its consecration until 1919. Paul Abadie died in 1884 and five different architects continued his work, the last of whom was Louis-Jean Hulot, who built the 84-metre (275-foot) bell tower in 1895 and was responsible for the monumental sculptures.

The façade's central statue by Eugène Benet is of Christ, while the two equestrian statues flanking it are St Louis and St Joan of Arc, by Hipplyte Lefèbvre. The dome is the second-highest point in Paris, after the Eiffel Tower. The interior is Byzantine in style, with squinches linking the ovoid dome to the square plan below. A colossal mosaic dominates the chancel. Designed by Luc Olivier Merson and Marcel Magne, it was constructed between 1912 and 1922. At 475 square metres (5,100 square feet), it is the largest in the world.

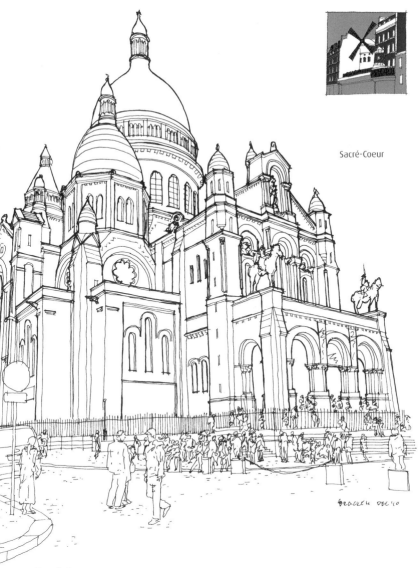

Sacré-Coeur

Sacré-Coeur

Opening times:

Basilica: 6am–10.30pm daily

Dome and crypt: 9am–5.45pm daily

Services: 7am, 11.15am, 6.30pm, 10pm Mon–Thur; 3pm Fri; 10pm Sat; 11am, 6pm, 10pm Sun

Website: www.sacre-coeur-montmartre.com

Tel: 01. 53 41 89 00

Did You Know?

The Sacré-Coeur bell tower contains one of the heaviest bells in the world, at 18.5 tonnes. Its clapper is a whopping 850 kilograms (1,900 pounds).

Montmartre

St-Pierre de Montmartre ❸

Follow rue Azaïs and turn right onto rue du Mont-Cenis. St-Pierre de Montmartre will be on your right at No. 2. Less visited than its more famous neighbour, this is actually a charming church and also one of the oldest in the city, having been founded as the Benedictine Abbey of Montmartre in 1133 by Louis VI and his wife, Adelaide of Savoy, who later became its first abbess and is buried here. The interior contains four marble columns, which supposedly come from the Roman temple that used to stand here. The choir is vaulted and dates from the 12th century. The nave was remodelled in the 15th century and the west front is from the 18th century. It was converted to a Temple of Reason during the Revolution – after the abbess was guillotined – but the church then fell into disuse, only being reconsecrated in 1908. Its Gothic stained-glass windows were destroyed by a World War II bomb and have been replaced by replicas. The church has a small cemetery, this is only open to the public one day a year on 1st November, All Saints' Day.

St-Pierre de Montmartre
Opening times: 8.45am–7pm daily
Tel: 01. 46 06 57 63

Place du Tertre ❹

The small square in front of St-Pierre de Montmartre leads into Place du Tertre. This charming square is filled with stalls selling art work and is lined with pleasant restaurants. *Tertre* means hillock in French, and this little hill is actually the highest point in Paris, 130 metres (430 feet) above the Seine. It wasn't always so jolly, however, as it used to be a site for public hangings. Artists began to frequent the area in the 19th century, and some of the restaurants even date from that time, with La Mère Catherine going as far

Place du Tertre

back as 1793. This was popular with Russian Cossacks at the time of Napoleon's defeat in 1814.

Later, in 1920, the house at No. 21 was the headquarters of the 'Free Commune', founded to perpetuate the area's Bohemian spirit – as if it needed any help. It is now an information centre on Montmartre. The **Espace Dali Montmartre** is located just off Place du Tertre, at No. 11 rue Poulbot. Simply follow the signs to this small museum which is home to 330 works by the Surrealist painter and sculptor. Its dark interior sets off to great effect the often bizarre nature of his work, the dramatic effect of which is further underscored by recordings of the artist's voice. The museum also contains a library.

Espace Dali Montmartre
Opening times: 10am–6pm daily
Website: www.daliparis.com
Tel: 01. 42 64 40 10

Did You Know?
The word 'bistro' for restaurant (which is sometimes also spelled 'bistrot') comes from the Russian word for 'quick' and dates from the time in 1814 when Russian soldiers swarmed into the city after Napoleon's defeat and used to bang on tables and shout it to get service.

Musée de Montmartre ❺
Return to rue du Mont-Cenis and turn left. Turn left again onto rue Cortot and the Musée de Montmartre will be on your right at No. 12. This fascinating museum tells the story of Montmartre from the days of the Abbey of St-Pierre de Montmartre right up to the present, with documents, drawings, photographs and other artefacts.

One of the finest houses in the area, it was the 17th-century home of the actor Roze de Rosimond (Claude de la Rose), a member of Molière's company who died, like Molière, during a stage performance of Molière's play *Le Malade Imaginaire* (*The Hypochondriac*). From 1875 it was used as a studio and living space by a number of artists, including Raoul Dufy and Pierre-Auguste Renoir. Maurice Utrillo also

Musée de Montmartre

lived here with his mother, Suzanne Valadon, who was a former acrobat turned artist's model who then turned out to be a talented painter herself.

Walk to the end of rue Cortot and turn right onto rue des Saules. You will see a small **vineyard** ahead of you on the right. Vineyards used to cover these hills in the Middle Ages, and this is the last of them. City authorities purchased this 2,000-square-metre (21,500-square-foot) plot in 1933 and planted a number of different varieties of grape, some of which are used in France's greatest wines, others of which have since all but disappeared from the shops.

Musée de Montmartre
Opening times: 11am–6pm Tue–Sun
Website: www.museedemontmartre.fr
Tel: 01. 49 25 89 37

Le Lapin Agile ❻

Continue along rue des Saules and you will come to Le Lapin Agile at No. 22. This intimate club was popular with artists and intellectuals at the beginning of the 20th century. It started out in 1860 as Au rendez-vous des voleurs (The Thieves' Rendezvous), also known as the Cabaret des assassins (The Assassins' Cabaret).

Bought by the entrepreneur Aristide Bruaud in 1903, it still retains much of the atmosphere of that time. It takes its rather odd name from the sign that was painted by André Gill in 1880. It shows a rabbit escaping a cooking pot, hence *Le Lapin à Gill* (Gill's rabbit) became *Le Lapin Agile* (the nimble rabbit).

Le Lapin Agile
Opening times: 9pm–2am Tue–Sun
Website: www.au-lapin-agile.com
Tel: 01. 46 06 85 87

Avenue Junot ❼

Continue along rue des Saules and turn left onto rue Caulaincourt. The entrance to Avenue Junot will be the second on your left. Turn right once you come to the avenue, which veers to the left and continues leftwards until you come out on rue Girardon. Near the beginning of this avenue (up the steps off the Allée des Brouillards) is the Château des Brouillards, a bizarre 18th-century house that was the home of 19th-century symbolist writer Gérard de Nerval. Avenue Junot was laid out in 1910 and includes many painters' studios. No. 13 has mosaics designed by Francisque Poulbot (who used to live here). He was famous for his pictures of Paris street urchins and is also credited with having invented a type of billiards. No. 15 is the Maison Tristan Tzara, named after the Roumanian Dadaist poet who lived here. The house's eccentric design, by Austrian architect Adolf Loos, was intended to reflect the poet's nature. No. 23 bis, the Villa Léandre, is part of a group of fine Art Deco houses.

Maison Rose

Moulin de la Galette

Turn right onto rue Girardon and the **Moulin de la Galette** will be at the bottom of the street on your right, overlooking the junction with rue Lepic. This is actually the Moulin du Radet, which now contains a restaurant called the Moulin de la Galette. There is another Moulin de la Galette further along the same side of rue Lepic, overlooking the junction with rue Tholozé. There used to be 14 windmills in Montmartre. These were used for grinding wheat and pressing grapes for wine-making. The Moulin du Radet and the Moulin de la Galette (originally built in 1622 and formerly known as the Blute-fin) both became dance halls at the end of the 19th century and provided inspiration for a number of artists, including Renoir and van Gogh. **Rue Lepic** is a popular shopping street and van Gogh used to live here at No. 54 in a third-floor flat.

Moulin de la Galette
Tel: 01. 46 06 84 77

Bateau-Lavoir ⑧

Walk down rue Tholozé and turn left onto rue Durantin, which turns into rue Garreau. Place Emile-Goudeau will be on your left. The Bateau-Lavoir faces out onto this small square at No. 13. This former piano factory gets its name from the fact that the building looked like the laundry boats that used to travel down the Seine.

Home to artists and poets from 1890 to about 1920, its residents included Picasso, van Dongen and Modigliani, who used to take turns sleeping in the beds and share the single tap. Picasso painted *Les Demoiselles d'Avignon* here in 1907, which is generally regarded as the first Cubist painting. The building burnt down in 1970 and a concrete replica has been built. Containing studio space for up-and-coming artists, it is closed to the public.

Did You Know?

The novelist Roland Dorgelès hated Modern art so much and was so tired of hearing the critic Guillaume Apollinaire praise it that he decided to play a practical joke in 1911. He borrowed the owner of the Bateau-Lavoir's donkey, tied a paintbrush to his tail and then gave the resultant 'artwork' the splendid title *Sunset over the Adriatic*. This was subsequently shown at a Salon des Indépendents. Sadly, however, history does not record what Guillaume Apollinaire's opinion of it was.

St-Jean l'Evangéliste ⑨ de Montmartre

Walk down rue Ravignan and turn left onto rue des Abbesses and you will come to **Place des Abbesses**. One of Paris' most picturesque squares is sandwiched between the rather dubious attractions of Place Pigalle, with its strip clubs

and threadbare erotica, and the Place du Tertre at the top of the hill, swamped with tourists hunting for local colour.

The Abbesses metro station was designed by architect Hector Guimard. These once-ubiquitous Art Nouveau station entrances can still be found dotted throughout the city.

Overlooking the square is **St-Jean l'Evangéliste de Montmartre**, the first church to be built using reinforced concrete. Designed by Anatole de Baudot, it was completed in 1904 and its interior contains some typically Art Nouveau flower motifs, while its interlocking arches suggest something a little more Moorish. Its workaday red-brick façade has earned it the less than glamorous nickname St-Jean-des-Briques (St John of the Bricks).

St-Jean l'Evangéliste de Montmartre
Opening times: 9am–noon, 3–7pm Mon–Sat, 2–7pm Sun
Tel: 01. 46 06 43 96

Chapelle du Martyre ⑩

Leave Place des Abbesses via rue Yvonne-Le-Tac and you will come to the Chapelle du Martyre on your right at No. 9. This chapel dating from the 19th century stands on the site of a medieval convent chapel, said to be the place where St Denis, the first Bishop of Paris, was beheaded for his Christianity in 250 CE. It was a pilgrimage site of major importance in the Middle Ages. The crypt of the original chapel was where St Ignatius Loyola, founder of the Jesuits, took his religious vows in 1534.

Chapelle du Martyre
Opening times: 10am–noon, 3–5pm Fri–Wed

Moulin Rouge ⑪

Retrace your steps along rue Yvonne-Le-Tac and turn left onto rue des Martyrs. Then turn right onto Boulevard de Clichy and the Moulin Rouge will be on your right at No. 82. The Cancan, that energetic high-kicking dance performed to the tune of Offenbach's *Orpheus in the Underworld*, is most often associated with the Moulin Rouge thanks to the iconic posters by Henri de Toulouse-Lautrec. Actually it originated on the other side of town, in Montparnasse, in the polka gardens on the rue de la Grande-Chaumière.

The Moulin Rouge was turned into a dance hall in 1900 and was home to the famous Dorriss Dancers, which included Yvette Guilbert and Jane Avril. This dance-show tradition lives on today, with the Las Vegas-style revue at the Moulin Rouge that includes high-tech lighting and magic shows.

Montmartre

Moulin Rouge
Dinner: 7pm
Shows: 9 and 11pm daily
Website: www.moulin-rouge.com
Tel: 01. 53 09 82 82

Cimetière de Montmartre ⑫

Continue along Boulevard de Clichy and turn right onto Avenue Rachel and the Cimetière de Montmartre will be straight ahead of you. Established by Napoleon, along with Montparnasse and Père Lachaise to clear downtown Paris of unhygienic old cemeteries, the Cimetière de Montmartre was established in 1798, and was extended to its present 12 hectares (30 acres) in 1825. Not as visited as some of the city's other graveyards, it is still a charming and evocative place to stroll.

Some of Paris' best-loved composers and writers are buried here, including Hector Berlioz and Jacques Offenbach, Alexandre Dumas *fils* and the German poet Heinrich Heine. The painter Degas, film director François Truffaut and Russian ballet dancer Vaslav Nijinsky are also buried here.

Nearby, close to Square Roland Dorgelès, is another smaller cemetery: **Cimetière St-Vincent**. This is the final resting place of the Swiss composer Arthur Honegger and the French artist Maurice Utrillo, whose paintings have done more to immortalise Montmartre's artistic legacy than almost anyone else.

Cimetière de Montmartre
Opening times: 8am–5.30pm Mon–Fri, 8.30am–5.30pm Sat, 9am–5.30pm Sun (closes 6pm daily in summer)
Tel: 01. 53 42 36 30

End of walks.

Further Afield

Further Afield

This chapter covers districts and specific buildings and places that are a little out of the city centre, or do not fall conveniently into any of the city walks. This includes places like La Défense, La Villette and Versailles, which are so large they are virtually walks in themselves. Then there is the spacious greenery of Cimetière du Père Lachaise, Parc des Buttes-Chaumont and Cité Universitaire, all of which are worth taking the time to stroll around. There are also individual buildings or monuments that simply cannot be missed, such as the Portes St-Denis and St-Martin, the impressive new Bibliothèque Nationale de France and the fascinating Manufacture des Gobelins. One building that simply has to be seen by anyone interested in Gothic architecture is the Basilique St-Denis, located just north of the city and not too far from the Marché aux Puces (flea market) of St-Ouen. This chapter begins, however, with two mini-walks through the west and north of the city, areas that both have a scattering of fascinating museums and houses, including the lavish Hôtel Salomon de Rothschild, the starkly Modernist Foundation Le Corbusier and the vast green expanse of the Bois de Boulogne.

THE WALK

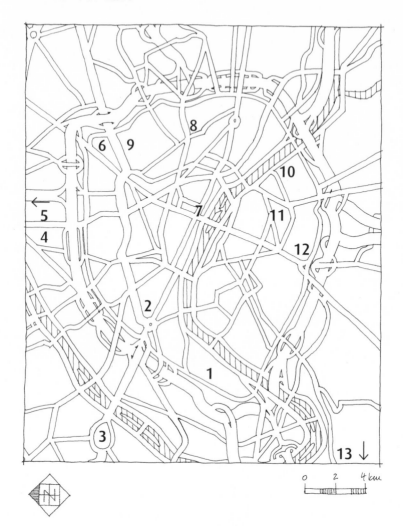

0   2   4 km

KEY

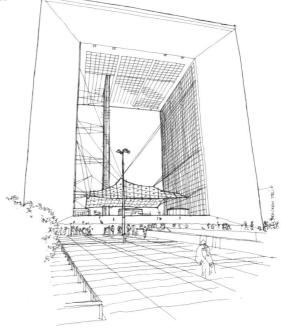

Further Afield

West ❶

Musée des Années 30

Metro: Marcel Sembat

Follow Avenue André Morizet and you will come to the Musée des Années 30 on your right at No. 28. This interesting museum was founded in 1998 in the Espace Landowski, an arts complex named after a sculptor who lived in the area from 1905 until his death in 1961. Several of Paul Landowski's works are on show in the complex which also includes a library and a cinema. The museum contains 800 paintings, 1,500 sculptures and 20,000 drawings, as well as furniture, ceramics and posters all dating from the 1930s. It also hosts temporary exhibitions.

Musée des Années 30
Opening times: 11am–5.45pm Tue–Sun
Website: www.annees30.com
Tel: 01. 55 18 46 42

Rue la Fontaine

Metro: Michel-Ange-Auteuil

The rue la Fontaine runs through a fashionable part of Paris and contains some of the city's most extraordinary early 20th-century architecture. No. 14 is Castel Béranger, or more commonly known as Castel Déranger (which means deranged), a stunning Art Nouveau apartment building designed by Hector Guimard using cheap materials to keep the costs as low as possible. Nicknamed the House of Devils because of its swirling figures, it established the architect's reputation and he went on to design the iconic entrances for the Paris metro.

Consisting of 36 apartments, the building's façade features redbrick, enamel tiles and red and white sandstone. The windows are arranged in a highly irregular pattern, while the metalwork is one of the building's most beautiful and striking features, especially on the balconies and over the entrance. The painter Paul Signac lived here. There are a number of other examples of Guimard's work on the street, including the Hôtel Mezzara at No. 60.

Foundation Le Corbusier

Metro: Jasmin

Walk up rue Jasmin and turn right onto rue Raffet, then right again onto rue du Docteur Blanche and the Foundation Le Corbusier will be on your right down the laneway at Nos. 8–10 Square de Docteur Blanche. Housed in the Villas La Roche and Jeanneret – the first two houses built by Le Corbusier in Paris, the Foundation was established in 1968.

Le Corbusier, or Charles-Edouard Jeanneret, was an immensely influential Swiss architect who lived and worked in Paris for most of his life. He was a

Foundation Le Corbusier

pioneer of the Modern Movement (also known as the International style or simply Modernism) and a gifted architect. He designed some flawless villas, such as the ones here, which despite seeming hard with their cold materials, actually contain warm and inviting interiors. His theories on urbanism, however, were less successful and have spawned many a damaging imitator, particularly his Plan Voisin, the 1920s' proposal to flatten the historic heart of Paris and replace it with massive tower blocks.

Le Corbusier's villas were part of a series of 'machines for living' that are dotted throughout the Paris suburbs. These two show the architect's trademark white concrete cubist forms, strip windows and stainless steel furniture. Both of these houses also stand on stilts.

Foundation Le Corbusier
Opening times: 1.30–6pm Mon 10am–12.30pm, 1.30–6pm Tue–Fri (to 5pm Fri), 10am–5pm Sat (Villa La Roche only)
Closed public hols, August, 24 Dec–2 Jan
Website: www.fondationlecorbusier.fr
Tel: 01. 42 88 41 53

Musée Marmottan – Claude Monet
Metro: La Muette
Leave La Muette metro station and follow Chaussée de la Muette. You will come to a little park and the Musée Marmottan will be on the other side of it, at No. 2 rue Louis Boilly. This museum is dedicated to the work of Claude Monet and is housed in the 19th-century mansion of art historian Paul Marmottan, who bequeathed the house and its priceless collections of Renaissance, Consular and First Empire paintings and furniture to the Institut de France in 1932. The

Further Afield

museum's focus changed after it received the Michel Monet bequest, which consisted of 65 paintings by the Impressionist Claude Monet (Michel's father). The collection includes some of Monet's most famous paintings, including *Impression – Sunrise* and several *Water Lilies*. Monet's personal art collection is also housed in the museum. This includes paintings by Pissarro, Renoir and Sisley.

Musée Marmottan – Claude Monet
Opening times: 11am–6pm Tue–Sun (to 9pm Tue)
Closed 1 Jan, 1 May, 25 Dec
Website: www.marmottan.com
Tel: 01. 40 50 65 84

Musée Dapper
Metro: Victor Hugo
Leave the Victor Hugo metro station and turn left up rue Paul-Valéry. The Musée Dapper will be on your left at No. 35 bis. This museum specialises in African art and culture and opened in 1986. It takes its name from a Dutch humanist who published an encyclopaedic description of Africa in 1668. It is also home to a world-class ethnographic research centre, the Dapper Foundation. This custom-built museum also contains an African-themed garden. With its emphasis on pre-colonial folk arts, particularly carvings, the museum's collections are a treasure trove of colourful and powerful African art. It also hosts music and dance performances and children's shows.

Musée Dapper
Opening times: 11am–7pm Wed–Mon
Website: www.dapper.com.fr
Tel: 01. 45 00 91 75

Musée de la Contrefaçon
Metro: Porte Dauphine
Located in an elegant town house at No. 16 rue de la Faisanderie, just off Avenue Foch, the Musée de la Contrefaçon is dedicated to the dubious art of counterfeiting. Established in 1951 by the Union des Fabricants, an organisation of French manufacturers, it seeks to expose the damage done by the making and selling of fake goods, something that has been going on since Roman times. Some of the fakes on display include watches, pens, luggage and clothes.

Musée de la Contrefaçon
Opening times: 2–5.30pm Tue–Sun
Closed public hols, August, 2 Nov
Website: www.unifab.com
Tel: 01. 56 26 14 00

Bois de Boulogne

Metro: Porte Maillol, Porte Dauphine or Porte d'Auteuil

This vast park covers 865 hectares (2,137 acres) and sits between the western edge of Paris and the Seine. It is all that remains of the vast oak forest of Rouvray, given by King Childeric II to the Abbey of St-Denis. Philippe-Augustus bought back the main part of the forest for use as a hunting ground and over the centuries it became the haunt of bandits, and it remained so even when François I built his fabled **Château de Madrid** here in the early 16th century (which has since vanished). The Compte d'Artois built the beautiful **Château de Bagatelle** in 1777, supposedly in 64 days to win a bet with his sister-in-law, Queen Marie-Antoinette. The Bois was turned into a park by Haussmann in 1852, who had it designed along the lines of an English park by Adolphe Alphand. The famous **Longchamp Racecourse** was built between 1855 and 1858 and the park was the location for the Summer Olympics in 1900. The Bois de Boulogne officially became part of the City of Paris in 1929. The northern part of it houses the **Jardin d'Acclimatation** which is an amusement park, while the **Pré Catelan** is a self-contained little park which boasts the widest beech tree in Paris. The **Bagatelle Gardens** contain a number of architectural follies and a famous rose garden, as well as the lovely château. The Bois is a sleazy red-light district at night and best avoided.

Bois de Boulogne
Open 24 hours daily

Bagatelle and Rose Gardens
Opening times: 9.30am, closing times vary from between 4.30 to 8pm depending on the season
Tel: 01. 40 67 97 00

Jardin d'Acclimiation
Opening times: 10am–7pm daily (Oct–May 6pm)
Tel: 01. 40 67 90 82

North ❷

St-Alexandre-Nevsky Cathedral

Metro: Courcelles

Leave the Courcelles metro station and walk down **rue Daru**. St-Alexandre-Nevsky Cathedral will be on your left at No. 12. This street is the heart of 'Little Russia'. Home to Russian émigrés for generations, they were either fleeing Tsarist or Soviet persecution and established a new life for themselves in this upmarket part of Paris. They established Russian schools and dance academies, as well as bookshops and traditional little tea shops.

The beautiful Russian Orthodox **St-Alexandre-Nevsky Cathedral** was designed by members of the St Petersburg Fine Arts Academy in 1861 and was jointly financed by Tsar Alexander II and the local Russian community. It forms a traditional Greek-cross plan and has five golden-copper domes. The rich interior mosaics and frescoes are Byzantine in style, and a wall of icons divides the church in two, originally to separate the male from the female worshippers.

St-Alexandre-Nevsky Cathedral
Opening times: 3–5pm Tue, Fri, Sun
Services: 6pm Sat, 10.30am Sun

Parc Monceau

Retrace your steps back up rue Daru and turn right onto Boulevard de Courcelles, Parc Monceau will be on your left. This charming park was established by the Duc de Chartres in 1778. He was a committed anglophile and commissioned amateur landscape architect Louis Carmontelle to design an English-style garden for him. Carmontelle, who was also a theatre designer, created a 'garden of dreams' and filled it with architectural follies.

The Duc was guillotined during the Revolution and the garden passed into state hands. About a third of it was redeveloped for housing, but the remaining 8 hectares (20 acres) were sold to the City of Paris in 1860 when it was redesigned by Adolphe Alphand, the designer of the Bois de Boulogne, and turned into a public park the following year. The site of a brutal massacre during the Paris Commune, it is now a pleasant place to stroll in and contains a number of charming structures, including a *naumachia*, or Roman-style pond flanked by Corinthian columns. This is based on the ornamental pools that the Romans used for simulating naval battles. There is also a rotunda designed by Nicolas Ledoux, which used to be a tollhouse.

Naumachia, Parc Monceau

Parc Monceau
Opening times: 7am–8pm daily (to 10pm summer)
Tel: 01. 42 27 08 64

Did You Know?
Parc Monceau was the scene of the first ever (successful!) parachute landing, made by André-Jacques Garnerin on 22 October 1792.

Musée Cernuschi

At the Avenue Velasquez side of Parc Monceau sits the Musée Cernuschi. This museum was founded in 1898 by Enrico Cernuschi, an Italian banker, in what used to be his home. It contains an impressive collection of Asian art, second only in quality and scope to the Musée Guimet. Cernuschi had collected about 5,000 objects, but these have grown over the years to be now about 12,500. Nine hundred or so are on display at any one time. Highlights include some ancient Chinese bronzes (15th to 3rd century BCE), Han Dynasty artefacts, Tang statues, Tang and Song ceramics and a large 18th-century Japanese Buddha.

Musée Cernuschi
Opening times: 10am–6pm Tue–Sun
Closed public hols
Website: www.cernuschi.paris.fr
Tel: 01. 53 96 21 50

Musée Nissim de Camondo

Walk down Avenue Velasquez and turn right onto Boulevard Malesherbes, then turn right onto rue de Monceau and the Musée Nissim de Camondo will be on your right at No. 63. This is the former home of Moïse de Camondo, a leading Jewish financier who commissioned architect René Sergent to build a facsimile of the Petit Trianon at Versailles in 1911. He wanted a suitable setting for his stunning collection of 18th-century furniture, tapestries, paintings and *objets d'art*. The house and its collection were bequeathed to Les Arts Decoratifs in memory of his son, who was killed in World War I. It opened as a museum in 1935. Sadly, his daughter and her family also suffered a horrible fate, being rounded up by the Nazis and sent to die in Auschwitz. The museum has been faithfully restored to resemble an 18th-century town house.

Musée Nissim de Camondo
Opening times: 10am–5.30pm Wed–Sun (last admission 4.30pm)
Closed public hols
Website: www.lesartsdecoratifs.fr
Tel: 01. 53 89 06 40

Further Afield

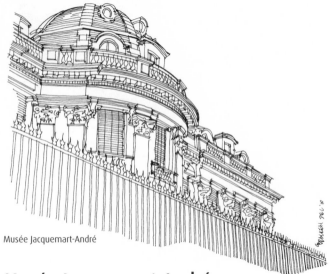

Musée Jacquemart-André

Musée Jacquemart-André

Continue along rue de Monceau and turn left at rue de Courcelles, then left
again onto Boulevard Haussmann and the Musée Jacquemart-André will be
on your left at No. 158. This imposing town house is home to an exquisite
collection of Italian Renaissance and 18th-century French works of art. It includes
frescoes by Tiepolo, paintings by Mantegna, Uccello, Boucher and Fragonard
as well as tapestries and furniture. These beautiful works were amassed by
19th-century collector Edouard André and his wife Nelie Jacquemart.

Musée Jacquemart-André
Opening times: 10am–6pm daily
Website: www.musee-jacquemart-andre.com
Tel: 01. 45 62 11 59

Hôtel Salomon de Rothschild

Walk back up Boulevard Haussmann and continue until you come to rue
Berryer, the imposing compound of the Hôtel Salomon de Rothschild will be
on your left at No. 11. Designed by Leon Ohnet and built between 1872 and
1878, this magnificent mansion with its extensive garden is located right in
the heart of the most fashionable district of Paris. Adèle Hannah Charlotte
Rothschild, widow of Salomon James de Rothschild, left the property to the
state in 1922, disinheriting her daughter, Hélène, for having married a Roman
Catholic. Today the building is home to a number of cultural institutions,
including the Centre Nationale de la Photographie.

Hôtel Salomon de Rothschild
Opening times: 12noon–7pm Wed–Mon
Website: www.cnp-photographie.com
Tel: 01. 53 76 12 31/2

Hôtel Rothschild

Musée Gustave Moreau
Metro: Trinité-d'Estienne d'Orves
Leave Place d'Estienne d'Orves via rue St-Lazare and turn left onto rue de la
Rochefoucauld. The Musée Gustave Moreau will be on your right at No. 14.
This was the home and studio of Gustave Moreau, a Symbolist painter best
known for his vivid, sometimes lurid paintings from the bible and mythology.
Jupiter and Semele, one of his best-known works, can be seen in this museum
which was established when the painter left his estate to the French state
after his death in 1898.

The collection comprises over 1,000 oil paintings and watercolours and more
than 7,000 drawings. It is also possible to visit the artist's private apartments,
although special permission is needed. These rooms have remained virtually
untouched since the artist's death and give an amazing glimpse into what
19th-century haute-bourgeois life in Paris must have been like.

Musée Gustave Moreau
Opening times: 10am–12.45pm, 2–5.15pm Wed–Mon
Closed 1 Jan, 1 May, 25 Dec
Website: www.musee-moreau.fr
Tel: 01. 48 74 38 50

La Défense ❸
Metro: La Défense Grande Arche
This is Paris' new business district, planned well outside the city so that the new
skyscrapers of the multinationals would not mar the city's venerable skyline.
Launched in the 1960s, it covers 80 hectares (200 acres) and is linked visually
and notionally to the city by the great axis that runs up the Champs-Elysées
from the Louvre – which is 10 kilometres (6 miles) away.

Further Afield

The area takes its name from a famous statue, *La Défense de Paris*, which dates from 1883 and commemorates the soldiers who defended Paris during the Franco-Prussian War of 1870–71. The focal point of the entire area is the Danish architect Johann Otto von Spreckelsen's **Grande Arche** (officially called the Grande Arche de l'Humanité or Great Arch of Humanity). One of President Mitterrand's Grands Projets, it opened in time for the bicentennial of the French Revolution in 1989. This 35-storey office building rises 110 metres (360 feet) into the air. Finished in granite and Carrara marble, it sits on a 100-metre-diameter (328-foot) square that is approached by a wide bank of steps. Glass lifts rise through tent-like 'clouds' that hang in the arch's vast open cube. Like the Louvre, the Grande Arche is rotated 6 degrees off axis, this is not done to mirror the Louvre, but so that the building's foundations would not interfere with the underground railway below. French architect Paul Andreu completed the building when Spreckelsen retired, it contains an exhibition gallery and a conference centre, and the roof commands superb views.

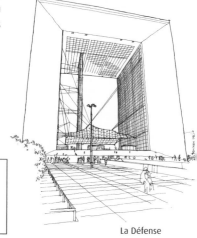

La Défense
Opening times: 10am–7pm daily
(Apr–Sept to 8pm)
Website: www.grandearche.com
Tel: 01. 49 07 27 27

> **Did You Know?**
> The void at the centre of the Grande Arche is so large that it could comfortably house the Cathedral of Notre-Dame.

La Défense

Marché aux Puces de St-Ouen ❹

Metro: Porte-de-Clignancourt

Leave the Porte-de-Clignancourt metro station and walk up Avenue de la Porte de Clignancourt. Pass under the Boulevard Peripherique and the Marché aux Puces de St-Ouen will be on your left at the beginning of Rue des Rosiers. This vast flea market, which covers 6 hectares (15 acres), is also Paris' oldest. Divided into specialist stalls, it is now most famous for furniture and decorative items, particularly from the Second Empire.

Clean and well organised, it is a far cry from the 19th-century rag-and-bone men who would tramp here from the city to sell their wares (they weren't allowed to do so within the city limits). By the 1920s this had turned into a proper market, and there have been tales of lucky browsers unearthing long-lost masterpieces. This does not happen so much today, although there are still some bargains to be had, if you are eagle-eyed and can haggle. There are more than 2,000 stalls to choose from.

Marché aux Puces de St-Ouen
Opening times: 9am–6pm Sat–Mon
Website: www.les-puces.com

Basilique St-Denis ❺

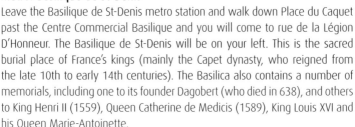

Metro: Basilique de St-Denis

Leave the Basilique de St-Denis metro station and walk down Place du Caquet past the Centre Commercial Basilique and you will come to rue de la Légion D'Honneur. The Basilique de St-Denis will be on your left. This is the sacred burial place of France's kings (mainly the Capet dynasty, who reigned from the late 10th to early 14th centuries). The Basilica also contains a number of memorials, including one to its founder Dagobert (who died in 638), and others to King Henri II (1559), Queen Catherine de Medicis (1589), King Louis XVI and his Queen Marie-Antoinette.

Consecrated as a cathedral in 1966, it began life as an abbey church in the 7th century, on what was purported to be the burial site of St Denis, the first Bishop of Paris, who was beheaded in Montmartre in 250 CE. He is now the patron saint of France. Abbot Suger, confidante of Kings Louis VI and VII, decided to enlarge the church around 1137 and rebuilt parts of it in a series of innovative new structural and decorative ways that helped create the first Gothic building.

The Basilica's nave is regarded as the prototype of the Rayonnant style of Gothic and was hugely influential throughout Europe. Replacing the heavy masonry walls of the old church with slender columns allowed plenty of light to enter through the greatly enlarged windows. Developments such as the pointed arch and flying buttresses also reduced the need for massive walls and so freed the interior space of columns and created the sensation of airiness and lightness that was the signature of this stunning new architectural style. Suger's changes were finished by 1144, and the rest of the church was rebuilt from 1231 onwards in the same beautiful style.

Basilique Saint-Denis
Opening times: 10am–6.15pm Mon–Sat, noon–6.15pm Sun, Apr–Sept; 10am–5.15pm Mon–Sat, noon–5.15pm Sun, Oct–Mar (last admission 15 mins before closing)
Services: 8.30am, 10am Sun
Tel: 01. 48 09 83 54

Did You Know?
Despite being the burial place for nearly every French king from the 10th to the 18th century, this was not where they were crowned. Coronations took place in the Cathedral of Reims.

Further Afield

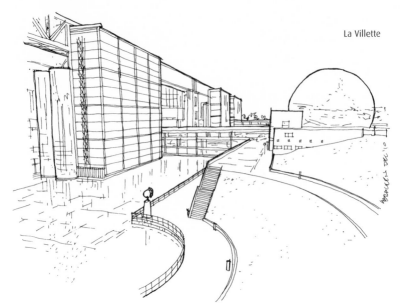

La Villette

La Villette ⑥

Metro: Porte de la Villette or Porte de Pantin

This is the largest park in Paris, covering 35 hectares (86 acres), and the second largest green space in the city after the cemetery of Père Lachaise. It was originally home to the La Villette slaughterhouses and livestock markets, which were closed down in the 1970s. The park's design is by Bernard Tschumi, and is the result of an international competition held in 1986. Consisting of 26 red follies scattered through 11 themed gardens, it houses the largest science museum in Europe. Tschumi's follies are linked to each other and the rest of the park via a series of landscaped walkways. They provide various services, including a children's workshop and a number of restaurants.

The Cité des Sciences et d'Industrie is a vast museum which is hugely popular with children because of its hands-on displays. Occupying the largest of the old abattoirs, architect Adrien Fainsilber created an imaginative high-tech, five-storey building that soars 40 metres (133 feet) into the air and covers more than 3 hectares (7 acres). The museum's main exhibit is Explora, a fascinating guide to the world of science and technology. There is also a children's science city, some cinemas, a science newsroom, a library and shops, not to mention the 260-seat Planetarium.

La Géode also contains a cinema, with an enormous 180-degree screen combining visual and sound effects to create a memorable experience. The Cité de la Musique is an elegant all-white complex that is home to a music conservatory, concert hall, library, music studios and a museum which contains more than 4,500 musical instruments, as well as works of art that illustrate the history of music since the Renaissance. The Zénith Theatre is a huge tent that is used for pop concerts. It can seat up to 6,000 spectators.

La Villette
Opening times: 10am–6pm Tue–Sat (7pm Sun)
Website: www.cite-sciences.fr
Tel: 01. 40 05 80 00

Portes St-Denis & St-Martin ❼
Metro: Strasbourg St-Denis

These are two city gates built into Charles V's old city wall by Louis XIV to commemorate his military victories. They replaced the medieval gates of a wall that has long since vanished. **Porte St-Denis** is located on the Boulevard St-Denis, at the junction where rue St-Denis turns into the rue du Faubourg St-Denis. Paid for by the City of Paris, it was built in 1672 to celebrate the King's victories on the Rhine and in Franche-Compté. Designed by architect François Blondel, it stands nearly 25 metres (80 feet) high and is based on the triumphal arch of Titus in Rome, with a central arch flanked by two smaller side arches and obelisks. The sculptural groups are by Michel Anguier.

Porte St-Martin is located on the other side of the Strasbourg St-Denis metro station, where Boulevard St-Martin crosses rue St-Martin. A heavily rusticated limestone-and-marble triumphal arch, it was built in 1674 to celebrate the same military victories as the Porte St-Denis, specifically the capture of Besançon (which signalled the defeat of the Triple Alliance: Spain, Holland and Germany). Designed by architect Pierre Bullet (a student of Blondel), it stands 18 metres (60 feet) tall and is decorated with some fine bas-reliefs.

Cimetière du Père Lachaise

Further Afield

Cimetière du Père Lachaise ❽

Metro: Philippe Auguste, Père Lachaise or Gambetta

The Philippe Auguste metro station is close to the cemetery's entrance on Boulevard de Ménilmontant, or you could take the Père Lachaise station which is close to one of the cemetery's side entrances. It is also possible to enter from the Gambetta station, whose entrance is close to the tomb of Oscar Wilde. This is Paris' most famous cemetery, it is also its largest. Built by Napoleon in 1804, it was laid out by Alexandre-Théodore Brogniart and covers 48 hectares (118 acres) on a wooded hillside. It must rank as the world's most visited graveyard.

One of a series established around the city, which included Montparnasse, Montmartre and Passy, Père Lachaise was initially thought to be too far out from the city centre and was as such not a popular burial place. Its popularity grew as the city spread. It takes its name from Louis XIV's confessor, Père François de la Chaise, who lived in a Jesuit house near here. Despite its initial unpopularity, it has been extended six times and contains some very famous graves, including writer Honoré de Balzac, composer Frédéric Chopin, actress Sarah Bernhardt and the singers Edith Piaf and Jim Morrison. Marcel Proust is also buried here while the remains of Molière and La Fontaine were moved here in 1817 to add a bit of glamour to the still new cemetery.

Cimetière du Père Lachaise

Opening times: 8am–5.30pm daily (from 8.30am Sat, 9am Sun, mid-Mar–early Nov to 6pm)

Tel: 01. 55 25 82 10

Did You Know?

Père Lachaise is officially called Cimetière de l'Est (Eastern Cemetery).

Parc des Buttes-Chaumont ❾

Metro: Buttes-Chaumont or Botzaris

At 25 hectares (62 acres), this is the third-largest park in Paris, and also one of the most surprising. It started from rather unpromising beginnings: a quarry that was being used as a rubbish dump overlooking a gallows. However, Baron Haussmann saw the potential of the hilly site and commissioned landscape architect Adolphe Alphand to convert it into a park in the 1860s. Others who worked on it included the engineer Darcel and a landscape gardener called Barillet-Deschamps. Together they created a lake, complete with a man-made island of real and artificial rocks, on which they placed a Roman temple. The park contains more than 5 kilometres (3 miles) of trails and walkways as well as several bridges. Apart from the island there are also cliffs, a grotto which encloses a 20-metre-high (65 feet) waterfall, and several gardens in different styles, including English and Chinese. The lake is popular with boaters, while children love the donkey rides.

Parc des Buttes-Chaumont
Opening times: 7am–8.15pm daily (1 Jun–15 Aug to 10.15pm; May and 16 Aug–30 Sept to 9.15pm)

Bibliothèque Nationale de France ❿
Metro: Bibliothèque F. Mitterrand or Quai de la Gare
France's National Library can be traced back to King Charles V's 14th-century royal library in the Louvre, which was opened to the public by Louis XIV in 1692. The library increased vastly during the Revolution, when the private libraries of aristocrats and clergy were added. The former King's Library was made a national amenity exactly one century after Louis XIV opened it to the public. Until recently it was housed in the beautiful but rather small rue de Richelieu building (see page 188), but President Mitterrand commissioned Dominique Perrault to design this impressive new complex in 1989. It opened in 1996 and acts as the repository for all the books published in France. It currently contains more than 10 million volumes.

This vast building is one of the cornerstones of the revitalisation of this formerly rundown part of the city. Its four glass towers sit atop a vast podium, containing the reference and research facilities where exhibitions are sometimes held of the collection's treasures. The four towers are supposed to represent open books, and this idea of openness is further reinforced by the use of glass throughout, although this has been somewhat less than ideal for the long-term storage of books.

Bibliothèque Nationale de France
Opening times: 9am–7pm daily (from 2pm Mon, from 1pm Sun)
Website: www.bnf.fr
Tel: 01. 53 79 59 59

La Manufacture des Gobelins ⓫
Metro: Les Gobelins
Located at No. 42 Avenue des Gobelins, this famous factory was originally established as a dye works by two brothers from Antwerp, Marc and Jerome de Comans, along with a fellow weaver called François de la Planche, who came from Oudenaarde in the Netherlands. These three men had worked for King Henri IV and established their tapestry factory here in an abandoned town house, the Hôtel Gobelin. Louis XIV's Finance Minister Colbert took it over in 1661 and moved most of the city weavers here to consolidate their work. Under the directorship of Charles Le Brun there were four workshops with as many as 250 weavers. Most were employed in providing furnishings for the king's new palace of Versailles.

The Revolution was a low point for des Gobelins, but it was re-established as a state enterprise under Napoleon III. Since 1861 it has concentrated on

Further Afield

La Manufacture des Gobelins

only making tapestries, no dyeing is carried out here any more. The building was destroyed by fire during the Commune of 1871, and this new, jauntily-symmetrical replacement was built in 1913, although some of the 17th- and 18th-century interiors have survived. Today, weavers continue working in the traditional way but produce more modern patterns, including designs by Picasso and Matisse.

La Manufacture des Gobelins
Guided tours only, 2pm and 3pm Tue–Thur (arrive 15 mins early), group tours by appointment.
Tel: 01. 44 08 52 00

Cité Universitaire

Cité Universitaire ⓬

RER: Cité Universitaire

Located at Nos. 17–21 Boulevard Jourdan, this campus was established in the 1920s for the thousands of foreign students who come to the University of Paris to study each year. The Cité Universitaire is a vast park through which are scattered 38 buildings in a variety of architectural styles – each linked to the country they represent. The Swiss House and the Franco-Brazilian House were designed by Le Corbusier, while the International House, which was donated by John D. Rockefeller in 1936, has a library, a restaurant and even a swimming pool as well as a theatre. The Cité Universitaire makes for a charming campus to stroll through.

Cité Universitaire
Website: www.ciup.fr
Tel: 01. 44 16 64 00

Versailles ⓭

RER: Versailles Rive Gauche

Leave the train station and follow the signs for the palace. Built by Louis XIV from the 1660s onwards, Versailles was the centre of political power in France. The sumptuous setting for the man known as the Sun King, it was and still is the largest palace in Europe. It could accommodate up to 20,000 people at a time. The château started out as a small hunting lodge used by the king's father, Louis XIII. Louis XIV was distrustful of Paris, having been traumatised by the mob as a child during the Fronde, and instead chose to establish his court well outside the city. Versailles wasn't just an egotistical reflection of the sovereign's might and majesty, it was also a very clever power ploy. By keeping the various aristocrats busy with piffling little issues related to court etiquette, the king was preventing them from getting up to mischief elsewhere, something that could have led them to challenge his authority.

The château

Louis Le Vau started to extend the original hunting lodge in the 1660s by constructing a series of wings that expanded into an enlarged courtyard. This was decorated with marble busts, antique trophies and gilded roofs. The garden side overlooked a great terrace from a naturally prominent position. Jules Hardouin-Mansart took over from Le Vau in 1678 and added the immense north and south wings, he also filled in Le Vau's terrace to create the famous Hall of Mirrors. The last thing he designed was the chapel, which was finished in 1710. Construction work continued throughout the rest of the 18th century, with the Opera House only being added in 1770. The equestrian statue of Louis XIV in the courtyard was placed there by King Louis-Philippe and dates from 1837. It stands where a gilded gateway once led into the **Royal Courtyard**.

Further Afield

This was separated from the **Ministers' Courtyard** by elaborate grillwork. The **Marble Courtyard** is decorated with marble paving stones, urns and busts and contains the gilded balcony of the King's Bedroom.

The interior

Charles Le Brun was responsible for the château's interior decoration. The private apartments of the king and queen were arranged around the Marble Courtyard, while the garden side contained the state apartments, which is where court life took place. The **King's Bedroom** is centred on the Marble Courtyard. Louis XIV died here in 1715, aged 77. The seven rooms that constituted the King's apartments were based on Apollo – Louis saw himself as the living embodiment of this ancient Greek god. Apollo was god of music, prophesy and healing. He is often thought to be the god of the sun as well, but this is inaccurate. Helios was the deity who drove the chariot of the sun across the sky every day. The **Salon d'Apollon** (Salon of Apollo) was Louis XIV's throne room. A copy of Hyacinthe Rigaud's famous 1701 portrait of the king hangs here. The **Hall of Mirrors** was the centrepiece of the state apartments. Stretching 70 metres (233 feet), its 17 huge mirrors face arched windows that look out over the gardens. This is where the Treaty of Versailles was signed in 1919, ending World War I.

The **Salon de la Guerre** (Salon of War) contains a stucco bas-relief by Antoine Coysevoix showing Louis XIV riding to victory. The **Queen's Bedroom** was where the Queens of France used to give birth, they did this in full view of the court. The Baroque two-storey **Royal Chapel** is located in the North Wing and was Mansart's last work. It was also Louis XIV's last addition to Versailles. It replaced four earlier incarnations, which were either destroyed or converted to new use.

The North Wing also contains a picture gallery and the **Opéra**, which was built in 1770 for the occasion of the marriage of the future Louis XVI to Marie-Antoinette. (This is usually closed to the public.) The South Wing was home to members of the higher nobility and was turned into a museum of French history by King Louis-Philippe.

The gardens

One of the world's great formal gardens, Versailles' geometrically arranged paths continue the Apollonian theme established in the king's apartments. Designed by Le Nôtre, and laid out between 1662 and 1690, the gardens are full of classical statuary and numerous smaller gardens, each with its own theme. The gardens' chief glory are the fountains, and there are many.

The Fountain of Latona features marble basins underneath Balthazar Marsy's statue of the goddess, while the Fountain of Neptune was designed by Le Nôtre and Mansart and contains lively groups of sculptures spraying spectacular jets of water. The Dragon Fountain features a winged monster, while the focal point of the entire park is the **Bassin d'Apollon**, a magnificent sculptural fountain showing the sun god starting his day's journey across the sky. Designed by Jean-Baptiste Tuby, the god's chariot rises out of the water accompanied by tritons and dolphins amid sprays of water. It is aligned on the château and faces the **Grand Canal**, which was the setting for Louis XIV's boating parties.

Other buildings

Louis XIV built the **Grand Trianon**, a small palace of pink marble, in 1687 as a place to escape the rigours of court life, and to spend time with his mistress, Madame de Montespan. It replaced an earlier pavilion, the Trianon de Porcelaine, which was named after the blue-and-white Delft tiles that covered its interior and exterior. Madame de Montespan fell out of favour and the palace was left to rot, but a year later the king decided to built a second trianon to house his new mistress, Madame de Maintenon.

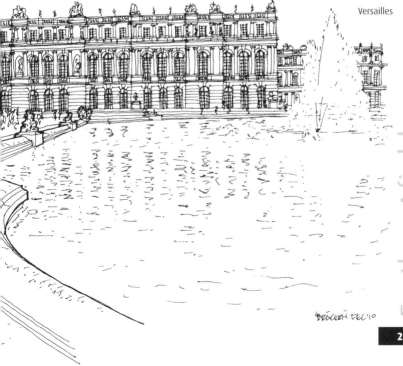

Versailles

Built by Jules Hardouin-Mansart, it was designed with great sensitivity to its surroundings, which it complements rather than dominates. Neither Louis XV nor Louis XVI liked it very much, although Napoleon was very fond of it. The **Petit Trianon** was designed by Jacques-Ange Gabriel for Louis XV in 1762, and was supposed to be the home of his mistress Madame de Pompadour. She died before it could be completed. It later became a favourite of Marie-Antoinette, who would escape here when she found the etiquette of the main palace too stuffy. All four facades are subtly different, with the west or principal front facing the king's garden being the richest, it features free-standing Corinthian columns.

Marie-Antoinette had landscape architect Antoine Richard lay out an English-style park nearby. Complete with lakes, lawns and rocky grottoes, it contains a Temple to Love by Richard Mique. Overlooking one of the lakes is the famous **Hameau**, or hamlet, the picturesque Norman style cottage-ornée farm buildings that the Queen had built so that she could play at being a shepherdess. It was here that she heard the ominous news that the Paris mob was marching towards the palace.

Versailles
Opening times: 9am–6.30pm Tue–Sun (last admission 5pm Nov–Mar, 6pm Apr–Oct)
Website: www.chateauversailles.fr
Tel: 08. 10 81 16 14

Grand Trianon
Opening times: Noon–7pm daily, Apr–Oct; noon–5.30pm daily, Nov–Mar

Petit Trianon
Opening times: Noon–7pm daily, Apr–Oct; noon–5.30pm daily, Nov–Mar

Events
Les Grandes Eaux Musicales (Apr–Sept)
Les Fêtes de Nuit (Aug–Sept)
Les Grandes Eaux Nocturnes (Sat during summer)

Architectural Styles

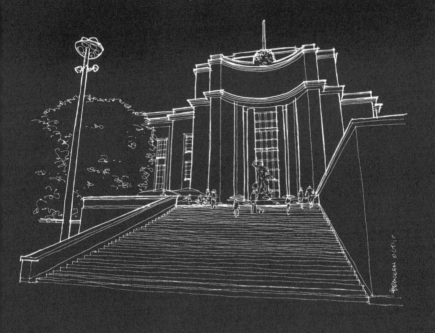

This chapter explains some of the architectural styles mentioned in the book, such as Beaux Art, which Paris is justifiably famous for, as well as the wider Neoclassical movement, of which Beaux Art formed a part. Along with the Gothic revival, Neoclassicism dominated the architecture of Europe and America (and the rest of the world through their colonial empires) in the 19th century.

This brief chapter also explains some other important stylistic movements such as Art Nouveau, which flourished around 1900 and Art Deco, which typifies the 1920s and '30s. Modernism, which developed around the same time as Art Deco, was a stricter, starker style, and one which came to dominate architecture for the rest of the 20th century. We begin with a much more ancient style, one which made a fleeting comeback in Paris in the last decades of the 19th century: Byzantine.

Byzantine

This style takes its name from the Byzantine Empire, the eastern half of the Roman Empire which continued for a thousand years after the western half had fallen to the Barbarians. Established in what is modern-day Turkey, the Emperor Constantine moved his capital from Rome to Byzantium in 306 CE and renamed it Constantinople. It remained the capital of the Byzantine Empire until it was reconquered by the Turks in 1453. (The name Constantinople was changed to Istanbul in 1919.)

Byzantine architecture is sumptuous and heady, as befits its Oriental origins. It makes use of luxurious materials, like marble and mosaic, as well as rich colours. One of its characteristic motifs is the use of the round dome over a square base. Concave triangular supports known as squinches enable the dome to fit over the square plan. This was used at Sacré-Coeur. Another example of a Byzantine style building is the St-Alexandre-Nevsky Cathedral.

Gothic

Also known as the Perpendicular style, the French not only invented Gothic but also created the most beautiful sub-genre of it, known as Rayonnant. It was developed in the early 12th century at the Basilique St-Denis just north of Paris. The Abbot Suger wanted to enlarge his church and had parts of it rebuilt in a new and innovative style. This was based on the desire to allow as much light to enter the building as possible. By replacing the heavy masonry walls of the church with slender columns, it allowed for much larger windows. Other structural innovations, such as the pointed arch and the flying buttress, also reduced the need for massive walls.

These structural and decorative innovations helped to create the first Gothic building, and the Basilique St-Denis is regarded as the prototype of the Rayonnant style. Its interior is free of columns, while its large windows help to create a sensation of airiness and lightness, something that characterised this stunning new style and which was quickly copied throughout Europe. The Sainte-Chapelle is another excellent example of this style.

By about the 16th century the Gothic style was dying out, the rediscovery of Classical architecture during the Renaissance helped ensure its demise. It experienced a strong revival in the 19th century, particularly in England, and one good example of this revival in Paris is the church of Ste-Clothilde.

Neoclassical

Classical architecture flowered in ancient Greece and Rome in the centuries before and after the birth of Christ. As a style, it was elegant and harmonious, but it disappeared with the fall of the Roman Empire. It was revived in the seventeenth century, firstly in Italy and then throughout the rest of Europe and North America, largely thanks to Andrea Palladio, an Italian architect who studied the ruins of ancient Rome and adapted their styles to suit his era. It makes use of the classical orders: Doric, Ionic and Corinthian are the three most important, with Tuscan and Composite rounding them out. Beginning in Greece in the 5th century BCE, and adapted by the Romans, these five orders have been the cornerstone of Neoclassical architecture ever since. A particularly fine example of the Neoclassical style is Claude Perrault's east front of the Louvre.

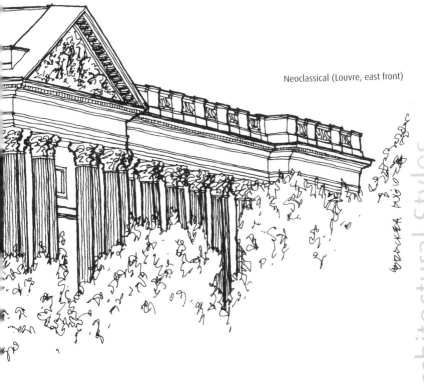

Neoclassical (Louvre, east front)

Architectural Styles

Beaux Art

This is an elegant French twist on the more solidly muscular Neoclassical style. Beaux Art may be lighter than normal Neoclassicism but it is equally strict about its academic references. It tended to make a point of amalgamating different historicist styles, yet its spatial expression remained highly conventional. This probably explains its popularity for grand buildings in the French colonies. Club houses and opera houses made lavish use of this style as it seemed a perfectly appropriate grand expression of the colonising culture. As a style it was also hugely influential in America, used for grand mansions and even some early skyscrapers. This is thanks to the many Americans who studied at the Ecole des Beaux Arts in Paris at the end of the 19th century. One attractive example of this style is the Grand Palais.

Art Nouveau

Brussels was the capital of the Art Nouveau movement, with the work of Belgian architect Victor Horta, but Paris has some beautiful examples of this undulating and sinuous style as well. Highly idiosyncratic, Art Nouveau flourished in Europe from the end of the 19th century to the outbreak of World War I. It made use of floral and organic motifs in highly stylised curvilinear designs.

Art Nouveau (metro station entrance, Place des Abbesses)

Highly expressive, Art Nouveau was also extremely versatile, being used for architecture, furniture, glass-making, textiles and even street furniture, such as Hector Guimard's gorgeous metro station entrances. It spawned regional variations, including Germany's Judendstil, the Secession style in Vienna and even individual geniuses such as Charles Rennie Mackintosh in Glasgow and Antonio Gaudi in Barcelona. Castel Béranger at No. 14 Rue la Fontaine (by Guimard) and No. 29 Avenue Rapp (by Jules Lavirotte) are other excellent examples of this style.

Art Deco

One of the most important cultural events of the 1920s was the Exposition des Arts Décoratifs et Industriels Modernes held in Paris in 1925. Known as Art Deco for short, this was the world's last total design movement, meaning that its streamlined elegance could be applied just as easily to a cigarette lighter or a luxury liner, or an apartment building or the piano in its penthouse. It was

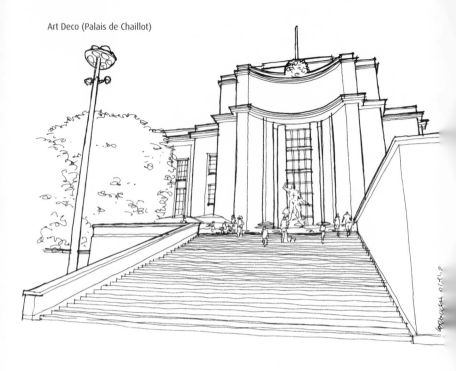
Art Deco (Palais de Chaillot)

also the first truly global style, and it expressed the aspirations and technical capabilities of the Modern age. The Palais de Chaillot is an excellent example of this sleek and streamlined style.

Modernism

This was really a social theory developed via architecture. The Modern Movement wanted to make society better prepared to meet the challenges of the modern era. Developed by architects such as Walter Gropius, Ludwig Mies van der Rohe and Le Corbusier in the first few decades of the 20th century, it wanted to eradicate historicism, ornament and anything that might distract from the business of living. It embraced innovations from industry and emphasised efficiency and hygiene to create 'machines for living in'. It was also known as the International Style.

Modernist buildings invariably used reinforced-concrete frames and were fitted with vast areas of glass. Their interiors were usually uncluttered. The style was popular for skyscrapers, and with the designers of social housing, particularly in the aftermath of World War II. It came to be criticised later in the 20th century for being too sterile and unresponsive to local context. Paris is home to some magnificent examples of the style in the form of two private villas by Le Corbusier, now home to the Fondation Le Corbusier, and the Maison de Verre by Pierre Chareau.

GLOSSARY

Apse   a recess, usually semi-circular, projecting from an external wall.

Arcade   a long arched gallery or veranda, often open at only one side, formed by a series of arches supported by columns or piers.

Arch   curved structure over opening.

Art Deco   style in art and architecture popular in the 1920s and '30s that drew inspiration from industrial elements.

Baroque   style of architecture in 16th- and 17th-century Europe which grew out of Renaissance Mannerism and evolved into the Rococo; typified by theatricality and an exuberance of plan and decoration.

Buttress   projecting wall support.

Byzantine   style associated with the Byzantine Empire (306–1453 CE).

Capital   head or top-most part of a column or pillar, often ornamental.

Chancel   the part of a church that contains the altar and sanctuary and often the choir.

Choir   in larger churches, the place reserved for the choir or singers, sometimes screened.

Colonnade   row of columns (similar to an arcade).

Column   a supporting element, always round in shape.

Corinthian order   the third of the Greek orders and fourth of the Roman; decorative, slender and elegant with two rows of acanthus leaves sprouting volutes or small scrolls.

Cottage-ornée   small dwelling in a park or the countryside, often asymmetrical and invariably picturesque.

Cupola   small dome.

Dome   a vaulted circular roof or ceiling.

Doric order   Classical order of architecture with distinct Greek and Roman varieties; simple in style, the Roman is less squat looking than the Greek, always fluted but invariably without a base.

Empire Neoclassical style of decoration that developed in France under Napoleon and heavily influence by ancient Greece, Rome and Egypt.

Faience earthenware covered with an opaque enamel coating, essentially a type of glazed terracotta.

Fretwork timber cut in a decorative and often repeating pattern.

Gable triangular upper part of a wall at the end of a roof.

Gargoyle waterspout on a parapet to allow water to flow from the gutter, often imaginatively carved in the form of demons or bizarre animals.

Gothic style of architecture in Western Europe from the 12th to the 16th century and again in the 19th, main features are the pointed arch, delicately carved stone and plenty of ornamentation.

Grotesque ornamental decorative carving, often of animals, flowers or mythological or fantastic animals.

Ionic order Classical order of architecture, the second in Greek and the third in Roman; easily identified by its capital with its rolled up scrolls; the Greek shafts are invariably fluted.

Loggia open-sided arcade, often on an upper floor.

Lunette panel on a wall under an arch or vault.

Mannerism architectural style of the late Renaissance (the 16th century), typified by its use of Classical elements in unexpected or surprising ways.

Monstrance a vessel used to display the consecrated Eucharistic host in certain religious ceremonies.

Motif design element which is repeated.

'ave the main body of a church, the place where worshippers sit.

'assical style of architecture popular from the 17th century onwards and based on the architecture of ancient Greece and the Rome; buildings are usually symmetrical, have elegant proportioning, and are characterised by the generous use of columns and pillars.

colonnades surrounding a building or courtyard.

an upright rectangular pier which looks like a pillar attached to a wall.

Pillar	a supporting element, always square in shape.
Plinth	plain continuous projecting surface under the base-mounting of a wall, pedestal or podium; the low plain block under a column or pillar in Classical architecture.
Portico	roof supported by columns or pillars, usually forming an entrance.
Reliquary	a shrine for keeping or exhibiting religious relics.
Romanesque	architectural style in Europe 7th to 12th centuries (between the fall of the Roman Empire and the advent of Gothic) characterised by heavy stone masonry and small round windows and doors with coarsened classical decorative features.
Rose window	a circular window popular in Gothic architecture, especially in larger churches or cathedrals, usually subdivided by complex radial tracery to form a floral pattern of great complexity and beauty.
Second Empire	style of architecture popular in France under Napoleon III (1852–70), it was essentially eclectic, borrowing from any number of different historical styles.
Terracotta	hard unglazed pottery used in decorative tiles, urns, statuary, etc.
Transept	any large division at right angles to the main body of a building (especially a church).
Tuscan order	one of the five Roman orders identified during the Renaissance, and along with the Doric the simplest and least decorative.

A Note on Language

Note: It is best to err on the side of formality when dealing with French people you don't know, for example in a shop, museum or restaurant. Use the *vous* form of address instead of the *tu*, a distinction which doesn't exist in English because there is no formal form of address. English people may confuse *vous* (formal) with *vous* (plural) which may result in them coming across as over familiar, something older French people will not feel comfortable with.

Glossary

FRENCH WORDS AND PHRASES

Conversation

Hello	*bonjour*
Excuse me	*excusez moi*
Do you speak English?	*parlez-vous anglais?*
I don't understand	*je ne comprends pas*
How are you?	*comment allez-vous?*
Good	*bien*
Goodbye	*au revoir*
I would like...	*je voudrais...*
Do you have...?	*avez-vous...?*
How much?	*c'est combien?*
Expensive	*cher*
Too big	*trop grand*
Too small	*trop petit*
Yes	*oui*
No	*non*
Please	*s'il vous plaît*
Thank you	*merci*
I don't want it	*je ne veut pas*
I'm sorry	*je suis desolee*

Directions

Excuse me	*excusez moi*
Here	*ici*
There	*là*
Where?	*où?*
When?	*quand?*
Closed	*fermé*
Left	*gauche*
Right	*droite*
Near	*près*
Far	*loin*
Entrance	*entrée*
Exit	*sortie*
North	*nord*
South	*sud*
East	*est*
West	*ouest*
Toilet	*les toilettes, wc*
Station	*la gare*
Museum	*le musée*
Church	*l'église*

Road	*rue*
Street	*rue*
Avenue	*avenue*
Boulevard	*boulevard*
Bridge	*pont*
Taxi	*taxi*
Bus	*bus*
Train	*train*

Numbers

1	*un, une*
2	*deux*
3	*trois*
4	*quatre*
5	*cinq*
6	*six*
7	*sept*
8	*huit*
9	*neuf*
10	*dix*
11	*onze*
12	*douze*
20	*vingt*
21	*vingt-et-un*
100	*cent*
1,000	*mille*

GENERAL LISTINGS

Gregory Byrne Bracken
www.gregory-bracken.com

Where Paris
www.wheretraveler.com

Bateaux-Mouches
www.bateaux-mouches.fr
Tel: 01. 42 25 96 10

Paris L'Open Tour
www.pariscityrama.com
Tel: 01. 42 66 56 56

Paris Version Française
www.parisvf.com
Tel: 01. 43 74 80 36

Tscoot
Email: book@TscOoT.com
Tel: 06. 60 45 00 20

LIST OF ICONS

Must See
Pages: 18, 20, 21, 23, 33, 48, 52, 61, 67, 72, 79, 82, 85, 87, 94, 99, 100, 112, 118, 121, 124, 132, 133, 134, 140, 145, 148, 149, 156, 159, 166, 167, 180, 182, 185, 192, 198, 216, 219.

National Monument
Pages: 18, 19, 20, 21, 23, 32, 33, 38, 39, 42, 48, 50, 51, 52, 55, 60, 61, 63, 70, 72, 73, 78, 79, 80, 82, 84, 85, 86, 87, 89, 94, 96, 99, 100, 102, 106, 108, 118, 121, 124, 131, 132, 133, 134, 140, 142, 144, 145, 147, 148, 149, 155, 156, 158, 159, 166, 167, 170, 172, 175, 180, 182, 184, 186, 187, 188, 192, 194, 196, 199, 204, 208, 211, 213, 214, 216, 217, 219.

Good View
Pages: 18, 21, 23, 48, 63, 67, 72, 79, 80, 82, 84, 100, 108, 109, 120, 121, 134, 145, 147, 148, 149, 154, 159, 166, 167, 173, 180, 182, 184, 192, 211, 219.

See At Night
Pages: 18, 23, 37, 38, 84, 85, 87, 94, 148, 149, 156, 166, 167, 182, 184, 192.

Drinking
Pages: 33, 37, 38, 48, 53, 61, 63, 69, 70, 85, 87, 89, 94, 96, 97, 112, 130, 131, 146, 155, 156, 159, 167, 169, 180, 181, 182, 184, 187, 194, 196, 198, 199, 208, 214.

Eating
Pages: 33, 37, 38, 48, 50, 53, 61, 63, 66, 69, 70, 79, 85, 87, 89, 94, 96, 97, 110, 112, 121, 124, 130, 131, 146, 156, 159, 167, 169, 170, 172, 180, 181, 182, 184, 187, 194, 196, 198, 199, 208, 214.

Shopping
Pages: 22, 33, 37, 38, 53, 55, 60, 61, 63, 69, 70, 85, 87, 89, 94, 96, 97, 112, 146, 155, 167, 169, 180, 181, 182, 184, 187, 194, 198, 204, 208, 212.

INDEX

index

Index

NOTES